Ball

Three in One

HB

HINKLER
BOOKS

First published in 2007
by Hinkler Books Pty Ltd
45–55 Fairchild Street
Heatherton, VIC 3202, Australia
www.hinklerbooks.com

© Hinkler Books Pty Ltd 2007

2 4 6 8 10 9 7 5 3
08 10 12 11 09

Printed and bound in China

HINKLER
BOOKS

ISBN 978 1 7418 1134 6

When exercising on the ball, always do the warm up exercises before attempting
any individual exercises. It is recommended that you check with your doctor
or healthcare professional before commencing any exercise regime. Whilst
every care has been taken in the preparation of this material, the Publishers
and their respective employees or agents will not accept responsibility for
injury or damage occasioned to any person as a result of participation in
the activities described in this book.

S I M P L Y
BALL

WITH PILATES PRINCIPLES

HINKLER
BOOKS

Editor: Margaret Barca
Creative Director: Ivan Finnegan
Photography: Peter Wakeman

CONTENTS

INTRODUCTION 5

THE BENEFITS 9

PRACTICAL MATTERS 10

CENTRING & BREATHING 12

BREATHING EXERCISE 14

POSTURE AWARENESS
& ABDOMINAL PREPARATION 16
Seated Balance, Pelvic Tilt, Chest Lift on the Ball

ABDOMINAL STRENGTHENING
& PELVIC STABILITY 22
Leg Pull, Chest Lift, Oblique Lifts, Roll Up Prep,
Double Leg Stretch, Single Leg Stretch

SPINAL MOBILITY & CONTROL 34
Side to Side, Pelvic Tilt, Rollover Prep, Rollovers

SPINAL ROTATION 42
Spine Twist

GLUTEALS & ADDUCTORS 44
Bottom Lift Series, Side Balance

SCAPULA STABILITY
& BACK STRENGTHENING 48
Arm Openings, Back Extension

FULL BODY INTEGRATION 52
Leg Beats, Push-ups

STRETCH & RELAX 56
Thoracic Push Through, Overhead Reach,
Hamstring Stretch, Hip Flexor Stretch

GLOSSARY 62

CONCLUSION 63

ABOUT THE AUTHORS 64

INTRODUCTION

The exercise ball, also known as the Swiss, Therapy, Physio, Fit, Balance, Gymnastic or Stability Ball, was originally used in Europe during the 1960s for the management of orthopedic and neurological problems. Physical therapists found that the ball's constant movement encouraged the individual to improve body and movement awareness, as well as call upon deeper layers of muscles necessary for overall joint stability, better posture and muscle balance. Use of the ball has extended from therapeutic applications to the sports medicine field and most recently to the general public in gyms and body-conditioning studios. The ball has become a versatile piece of exercise equipment. It can act as an aid to support the body weight and facilitate stretching, decrease stability at various angles to promote optimal strengthening of the whole body, or simply add new dimension and dynamics to any exercise regime. Strengthening the body in this way has been found to benefit the individual so that everyday activities or sporting endeavours are enhanced by improved movement mechanics, balanced strength of both sides of the body and faster reflex.

Exercising with the ball shares similarities with the principles behind the Pilates Method, which is a movement system that focuses on body alignment, balanced strength and movement control. The Method was developed by German-born Joseph Pilates in the early 1900s and he used his knowledge of the body to rehabilitate injured soldiers during World War I. He later opened an exercise studio in New York where he worked one-to-one with his clients, addressing their particular postural and structural needs. Pilates exercise sequences have endless scope for movement possibilities, ranging from a basic rehabilitative level to more advanced manoeuvres requiring greater athleticism and coordination. Many people worldwide enjoy the multi-dimensional qualities of the Pilates approach to exercise. The dynamics of the Method vary between studios and instructors, though the principles remain the same. It is a proven technique of developing and maintaining physical strength and mobility. It has a solid record of success with people of all ages and fitness levels and is adaptable to ever-evolving refinements in physical conditioning techniques.

INTRODUCTION

The powerful fundamental principles of Pilates need to be understood and applied in order to achieve the most from practising this technique.

CONCENTRATION
Visualisation and mental focus are essential to gain muscle control.

CONTROL
Quality movement is most beneficial and less harmful to joints and muscles.

CENTRING
The abdomen, lower back, hips and buttocks, or the 'powerhouse', is the primary focus of strength, stability and 'core' control.

FLUIDITY
Graceful, flowing motion is required, with no static, jerky or rushed movements.

PRECISION
Purposeful movement with good body alignment develops better muscle patterns for everyday activities.

BREATHING
Applying a breathing pattern assists movement rhythm and control, as well as energising the whole system.

Blending the ball into a series of Pilates floor movements is a simple progression because the principles remain the same. The concept of torso stability and coordinating breath and abdominal control also apply when using the ball. As an unstable base, the ball can help the individual gain greater awareness of where they are in space, assist them in concentrating on the exact purpose of the exercise and especially focusing on a strong 'core'. Merely sitting on the ball has benefits for muscles otherwise unused, as well as promoting circulation with the constant adjustment of position needed to maintain an ideal posture. Balancing on the ball also encourages the muscles to release tension so that they can gain strength in a more effortless manner. The ball lends itself well to exercises that provide gentle stretching and movement of the spine in particular and Joseph Pilates used to declare that an individual is as young as his spine is flexible!

THE BENEFITS

Now that many of us are finally steering away from the 'no pain, no gain' mentality of getting fit, patient measures can be taken to practise a more holistic way of developing control over movement, posture, physical vitality and, of course, the way we look. Incorporating the Pilates principles in your ball workout will enable you to develop overall body strength and tone rather than isolating larger muscle groups that are possibly already strong. We move about every day using our whole body and we should exercise with that in mind. Balancing on the unstable ball reinforces the focus of using the deep abdominal, back and pelvic muscles as the primary base of support for the torso. The 'centre', 'core' or 'powerhouse' will be strengthened and become more reliable for pelvic and spinal support during general daily activities. Having this area stronger and more stable will also enable you to have greater control over your limb movements. As the workout is mostly always moving—never static—further benefits include muscle endurance, greater coordination, poise and gracefulness.

Time spent exercising effectively is a wise investment in your physical future. Your exercise regime should provide you with functional results as well as being enjoyable and a 'break away' from your daily grind.

Exercising with the ball is one way to eradicate boredom, monotony or frenzy that many people associate with a workout. In order to exercise effectively for your health and perhaps reignite your enthusiasm for your efforts, you need to think of what you wish to achieve. Then, when you have an intention, you will exercise with purpose and over time you will accomplish positive results. Even if you already have an established fitness routine, it's possible to become stale which will result in loss of focus and concentration. Joseph Pilates believed that mindful intention behind a movement was the key to developing muscle control, correcting postural imbalances and restoring energy levels. The aim is intelligent exercise.

Anyone can grab an exercise ball and execute ten or more stomach 'crunches'. What makes this workout different is the inclusion of Pilates fundamentals. The technique is so precise and focused that correct execution becomes a physical discipline much like dance or martial arts. This physical training is unique with its emphasis on lengthening muscles while strengthening them, stabilising the lumbar spine and pelvis while movement of the limbs and upper torso is fluid, and controlled breathing which provides a rhythm and facilitates deep abdominal connection.

PRACTICAL MATTERS

Every person has different needs when exercising and you should aim for the ideal posture and muscular balance for your own physique. Primarily, always ensure that you keep your deep abdominal muscles lifted and drawn in towards your lower back. Never grip your muscles. Think of them like sponges that you gently squeeze, press, stretch or lengthen. How you perform each movement is the essence of what Pilates body conditioning is—understand the aim of the exercise, focus on the part of you that is stable and the part that is moving smoothly. Work your body from the core out, instead of relying on the superficial muscle layers. Remember that there is no real benefit in dozens of thoughtless repetitions in a vain attempt to achieve a beautiful body. 'Less is more', with a maximum of 6–10 repetitions being sufficient for each exercise. Be consistent with a slower pace with greater attention to accuracy and control. Practising your ball workout three to four times a week is good, depending upon your other activities, though certainly try to spend time daily on a few of the initial exercises that will reinforce the principles for you. This sensible approach to your body-conditioning regime is like 'building blocks'—you will gradually add dimension to your exercises, layer upon layer, developing your ability to perform movements with ease and grace.

If you have an injury—past or present—or if you are pregnant or post-surgery, it is strongly recommended that you consult your doctor or physical therapist before embarking on any exercise program. Remember that some of the following exercises may be unsuitable for your body and you may have to modify them, or avoid them.

REQUIREMENTS

Quality exercise balls are available through various distributors, in particular medical supply and sporting good outlets. Ideally choose one regarded as 'burst-resistant' for

greater safety, durability and shape integrity over time. They are generally available in a variety of sizes and colours. The appropriate size for you is one that allows your hip joints to be angled slightly higher than your knees when you are seated on the ball. A ball too small will disturb your neutral spinal and pelvic alignment and one too large will become too difficult to control during your workout. Balls are inflatable with various pumps. The first time you inflate your ball don't fill it completely and let it settle for

some hours before increasing the firmness. A softer ball will give you more support and stability; if inflated too hard it may be uncomfortable and too difficult for you to balance on.

Wear clothing that is comfortable and won't restrict your movement. Exercise on a mat for some spinal support and when you are lying on the ball ensure that it doesn't slip on the floor surface.

CENTRING
& BREATHING

The following three concepts should become a central focus for you throughout your ball workout. They are the foundation of the Pilates principles and will aid you in correct and intended execution of each exercise.

NEUTRAL PELVIS POSITION

The pelvis is a base of support for the spine and when it moves there are direct repercussions for the spinal curves. When the pelvis tilts forward or backward the position of the lower back, in particular, changes. Ongoing clinical research into the prevention and management of back pain demonstrates that maintaining the natural curvature of the spine is necessary while developing strength and endurance of the deep abdominal and paraspinal muscles associated with achieving 'core stability'. While practising Pilates and ball exercises a 'neutral pelvis' position is the ideal basis for correct spinal alignment. This position is easy to find when lying on your back if you relax your hip and back muscles so that no tilt of the pelvis occurs. Your two hip bones (iliac crests) and your pubic bone all form a parallel level with the floor. Think of the back of your pelvis as an anchor point while on the floor, so that you develop a feeling of stability through your centre. When sitting, standing or lying on your back, side or front, you should be able to develop the same corset-type stability with this alignment intact. When sitting, be right on top of your sitting bones to help you find your Neutral Pelvis position—you'd feel these if you were to sit on a hard surface, as they are the lowest boney protrusions of the pelvis.

CORRECT ABDOMINALS

The Pilates approach to abdominal strengthening was originally aimed at achieving greater support for the back and pelvis. Joseph Pilates' technique of maintaining a stable pelvis and lumbar spine while flattening the abdomen firmly during leg and upper torso movement corresponds with current methods of 'core stabilisation'. The action of the abdominals during this process must entail a broadening and flattening sensation of the lower abdominal region while also lifting or drawing up the muscles of the pelvic floor, which support the bladder. Typical expressions of such instructions during a Pilates workout include 'scooping', 'hollowing', 'navel to spine', 'draw in and up' or 'zipping', among others. The idea is being able to visualise internally how your lower abdominals are acting in order to help stabilise your pelvis and reinforce your spine. It is appropriate for everyone to focus on strengthening the deeper muscles of the abdomen so that other muscles—in particular, hip and lower back muscles—don't become dominant and overtight.

BREATH CONTROL

How you breathe while executing the exercises will determine how well you develop muscle control and stamina. The

Pilates technique of breathing requires you to breathe laterally, which means expanding the side and back of the lower ribcage while taking in air. This will enable you to still focus on the abdominal muscles drawing inward and upward toward your spine. Purposeful breathing throughout exercising will also create an even working pace and assist you in maintaining full control of each movement. You should not over-emphasise deep breathing, but simply be aware of this breathing technique while you learn to coordinate accurate movements with correct abdominal patterning. Breathing should be calming and assist you in releasing tension from the muscles you don't need to use while you focus on improving your posture and general wellbeing.

PREPARATORY NOTE

Embody these three basic postural essentials and gradually learn to coordinate movement while managing these subtle changes. Start to become aware of the alignment of your body as a whole structure—your Neutral Pelvis position, the natural curves of your spine, your hip, knee and ankle joints in line, your shoulder blades gently held back and flat against your ribs, your chin gently lowered and the back of your neck lengthened upward. This will help you understand the intentions behind the Pilates principles and the Simply Ball Workout. More

importantly, these ideas should provide you with a basis for restoring posture and balance to your everyday life.

BREATHING EXERCISE

Purpose To establish the three basic postural concepts while lying on the floor, or seated on the ball. Create an awareness of where your pelvis and spine are positioned in a neutral alignment and learn how to coordinate a lateral breathing technique with a strong sense of your deep abdominal muscles supporting your back. Begin every exercise with this same preparation and incorporate these principles throughout your ball workout. This practice will soon become second nature as you focus all your movements around a strong and stable centre.

1 Lie on your back with your heels on the ball, knees and ankles slightly apart. Position your knees vertically above your hips and place your hands on your lower abdomen.

2 Establish a calm breathing pace, just as you would normally breathe, while maintaining an awareness of your Neutral Pelvis position and relaxed neck and shoulders. Breathe in, count four. Breathe out, count four. Repeat for a moment.

3 Now, continue the lateral breathing pattern and begin scooping your lower abdominals deep toward a central spot in your mid-lower back. You may place your hands on your ribs to be more aware of the sideways breathing action. Maintain the lift of your pelvic floor each inhale and re-emphasise the navel-to-spine action with each exhale.

4 Then practise this posture and lateral breathing pattern while seated on the ball. Make sure you are sitting on your 'sitting bones' rather than being too far back on the ball and allowing the backs of your thighs to bear your body weight.

POSTURE AWARENESS & ABDOMINAL PREPARATION

Purpose *To establish a neutral alignment of the pelvis and spine while seated on the ball and learn balance and efficient posture control so the body's musculature does not overwork. Also, incorporating small movements of the lower and upper torso for abdominal warm-up.*

SEATED BALANCE

1 Sit on the ball as though you are seated in a straight-backed chair, with your feet no more than hip-width apart. Maintain a Neutral Pelvis position, draw your navel toward the spine and lengthen your waist. Feel as though you're weightless and buoyant, so you don't slouch into the ball. Try to limit the use of your feet and legs to stabilise your body.

2 Lift one thigh as you inhale and lower it as you exhale. Concentrate on the stability of your opposite hip and waist. Alternate legs so you become accustomed to transferring your weight while thinking of your centre. Remember not to lose your 'straight-backed chair' posture.

3 Repeat 10 times, alternating legs. Place your hands behind your head for further challenge.

NOTE

Try to find your sitting bones—the hard 'bottom bones' you would be aware of if you were to sit on a hard surface. Think of these as your 'feet', when you're not standing on your feet. So, make sure that you distribute your body weight down through your sitting bones, rather than through the back of your thighs.

Posture Awareness & Abdominal Preparation

(continued)

Pelvic Tilt

1 Inhale, lengthen your lower ribs up away from your hips and scoop your abdominals firmly toward your spine. Maintain your natural spinal curvature.

2 As you exhale, further scoop your abdominals and roll your pelvis back into the ball. Keep your ribcage fairly still in space as you roll your tail under, rounding your lower back.

3 Hold still as you inhale—remember your lateral breathing pattern—and reverse the roll as you exhale so as to resume an erect posture. Lengthen the front and back of your waist area equally so you don't end up over-extending your spine.

4 Repeat 4–6 times.

5 Following your last repetition, roll your pelvis under and walk your feet forward so you can lie back on the ball to prepare for Chest Lift on the Ball.

Posture Awareness & Abdominal Preparation

(continued)

Chest Lift on the Ball

1 Make sure that your back, from the tips of your shoulder blades to the back of your pelvis is in contact with the ball. Place your hands behind your head and have your feet no more than hip-width apart to promote good knee alignment.

2 With your hands supporting the head and neck lean back partially, scoop your abdominals and inhale to prepare. Imagine aiming your lower abdominals towards the back of your pelvis—a couple of inches below 'belt-line'.

3 Exhale as you curl your shoulders off the ball. Keep the tips of your shoulder blades just on the ball and deepen your abdominal scooping. Hold still and inhale laterally—don't release your lower back.

4 Exhale, lowering your shoulders back toward the ball. Especially keep your back and abdominals strong here. Inhale, prepare again.

5 Repeat 4–6 times.

6 Change the breathing pattern. Exhale as you curl and inhale as you lower, so there is no stopping and coordination is challenged. Keep the lower half of your torso absolutely still and strong while the shoulder girdle is free to move. Remember breathing laterally will assist you in scooping ever-so-strong lower abdominals.

7 Repeat 4–6 times.

ABDOMINAL STRENGTHENING & PELVIC STABILITY

Purpose *To develop a strong and stable mid-section. This is the essence of the Pilates method, executing various limb and upper torso movement to work the deep abdominal muscles and challenge the stability of the pelvis and lumbar spine.*

LEG PULL

1 Lie on your back with your heels on the ball, slightly apart, and knees vertically aligned with your hips. Maintain a Neutral Pelvis position and place your hands on your hips. Breathe laterally and scoop your abdominals.

2 As you inhale allow the ball to roll away, not completely straightening the legs. Maintain your abdominal bracing and back stability.

3 Draw the ball back toward you as you exhale. Emphasise each drawing in action of the legs, ensuring your abdominals reinforce the spine in its neutral position.

4 Repeat 4–6 times.

PROGRESSION

Keep a stable back as you now move double time—inhale for the 'in' and 'out' movement and exhale as you do the next 'in' and 'out'. So, the legs may move a little quicker, but your breathing stays calm and controlled—as do your abdominals, scooping straight to your spine. Try to have a mental picture of what body part is strong and still and what is free to move. This is a key fundamental in learning how to embody Pilates principles. Repeat 4–6 times

ABDOMINAL STRENGTHENING & PELVIC STABILITY

(continued)

CHEST LIFT

1 Begin as for Leg Pull and place your hands under your head and neck. Breathe in, focusing navel to spine. Use this preparation at the beginning of all your abdominal exercises.

2 Exhale as you curl your head, neck and shoulders just clear of the floor. Emphasise your scooping abdominals and stable back and pelvis.

3 Inhale laterally as you lower back to the floor with control. There should be absolutely no release of the lower back as you lie back to the floor. Remember that the role of your abdominals is to reinforce the front side of your spine.

4 Repeat 4–6 times.

PROGRESSION
Begin with your legs extended away from you and as you curl your head and shoulders off the floor pull both legs toward you. Repeat 4–6 times.

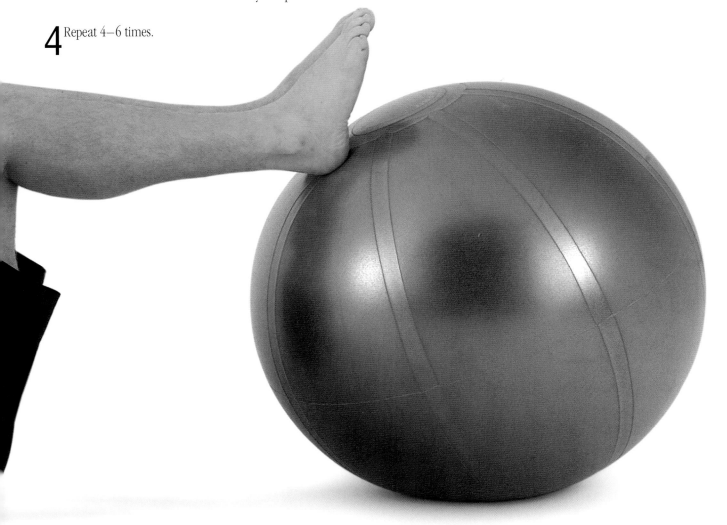

ABDOMINAL STRENGTHENING & PELVIC STABILITY

(continued)

OBLIQUE LIFTS

1 Begin as for Chest Lift. Inhale as you prepare your abdominals. Stabilise the pelvis and lower back.

2 As you exhale lift the head and shoulders, rotating your upper torso so that you aim one shoulder to the opposite hip. Maintain a stable Neutral Pelvis and focus on the side of the waist that you twist towards. Imagine 'pinning' your waist to the floor.

3 Inhale as you lower—keep your abdominals scooping all the while as this is essentially a preparation for your next repetition.

4 Alternate sides, 4–6 times.

PROGRESSION

Begin with your legs extended and add the Leg Pull as you did with Chest Lift. Ensure that your legs don't come closer to you than a 90-degree angle with your hips. Alternate sides for 4 repetitions.

Abdominal Strengthening & Pelvic Stability

(continued)

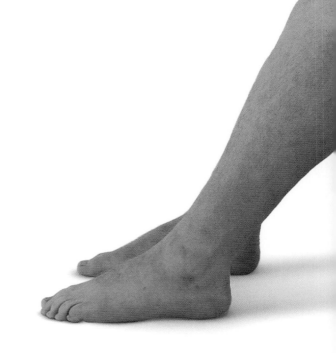

Roll Up Prep

1 Begin lying on your back with your legs bent, knees and feet slightly apart. Reach your arms to the ceiling and lightly squeeze the ball between your hands. Draw your shoulders down and secure the back and pelvis by scooping your abdominals. Breathe in.

2 Exhale, lifting your head, neck and shoulders and reaching the ball beyond your knees. Focus on your abdominals—imagine your navel-to-spine action scooping right up under your ribs. Inhale, hold strong and still.

3 Exhale as you roll back to the floor with control, pressing your abdominals inward and upward.
Finish with the ball reaching for the ceiling.

4 Repeat 5 times.

ABDOMINAL STRENGTHENING & PELVIC STABILITY

(continued)

DOUBLE LEG STRETCH

1 Begin lying on your back with your feet on the ball, knees bent and aligned over your hips. Place your hands behind your head and neck. Start the exercise as though doing a Chest Lift. Inhale, prepare.

2 Curl your head, neck and shoulders off the floor as you exhale. Scoop your abdominals.

3 Inhale, push the ball away and exhale as you draw it back toward you. Repeat the leg pull 4 times in all, then inhale to hold still and strong.

4 Exhale as you lower your head and shoulders. Maintain constant control of your back, pelvis and abdominals—try not to focus primarily on the ball.

5 Repeat all for 2 sets.

PROGRESSION

Begin in the same position, though place your hands on your knees. Lift your head and shoulders on the exhale and when you inhale, push your legs out and extend your arms up by the sides of your head, so that toes and fingers reach in opposite directions. Take great care not to release your back and stomach. Emphasise the exhale, when you circle the arms and 'pull' your knees and hands back together. Try to imagine your abdominals do the 'pull'—your centre stays absolutely strong and the back of your pelvis remains anchored to the floor. Repeat all for 2 sets.

ABDOMINAL STRENGTHENING & PELVIC STABILITY

(continued)

SINGLE LEG STRETCH

1 Start lying on your back with both legs in the air, knees bent at a 90-degree angle to your torso. Reach your arms to the ceiling with the ball between your hands. Breathe in, drawing your stomach to your spine and your shoulders down. Squeeze the ball slightly.

2 Exhale as you extend one leg upward and away from you, maintaining abdominals.

3 Inhale as you draw the leg back in. Repeat on the other side.

4 Continue to alternate sides with 6–10 repetitions. Try to emphasise scooping your abdominals upon each inhale because this gives you a stronger sense of stability before you extend the next leg.

PROGRESSION

For additional abdominal work, curl your head
and shoulders off the floor throughout. Squeeze
the ball a little and draw shoulders down and
abdominals in. Alternate legs for 6–10
repetitions.

Spinal Mobility & Control

Purpose *To promote controlled movement of the spine for strength, segmental coordination and greater mobility.*

Side to Side

1 Start with your spine and pelvis in a neutral alignment and the ball directly under your legs, making contact with both your thighs and calves. Once again, your knees are vertically aligned over your hips. Place your arms, palms up, at a moderate distance away from your trunk.

2 Prepare your abdominals and maintain throughout the exercise. Anchor your shoulder blades to the floor so you don't rely on your arms to stabilise you. Inhale as you roll onto one side of your pelvis.

3 Exhale as you return to the centre, ensuring it is your waist muscles that move you. Try not to lead the movement with your legs or back.

4 Alternate sides for 8–10 repetitions.

Spinal Mobility & Control

(continued)

Pelvic Tilt

1 Lie on your back with your feet on the ball and your spine and pelvis relaxed in a neutral alignment. Place your arms, palms up, slightly away from your torso, scoop your lower abdominals in and up. Inhale.

2 Exhale as you further draw your abdominals inward to initiate a pelvic tilt backward, stretching your lower back. Ensure that your knees are pointing directly up toward the ceiling and that the backs of your thighs assist with the movement.

3 Inhale laterally, holding the position. Feel the lower part of your gluteals lifting you.

4 Exhale as you roll back to the floor with control, relaxing your hips completely at the end of the roll. Try to keep the ball still throughout and focus purely on mobilising and smoothly articulating your lower back.

5 Repeat 3–4 times.

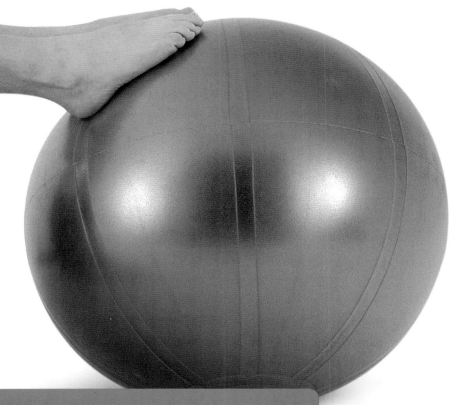

PROGRESSION

For additional legwork and to challenge your stability, try rolling off the floor a little further (exhale) and extending your legs away from you at the top of the movement (inhale). Exhale as you pull the ball back—buttocks high and knees pointing skyward—inhale to hold and maintain. Exhale as you roll and recover. Focus on the lower gluteals and your abdominals. Repeat 3–4 times.

SPINAL MOBILITY & CONTROL

(continued)

ROLLOVER PREP

1 Begin lying on your back with the ball between your calves and ankles. Extend your legs toward the ceiling. Emphasise a Neutral Pelvis, scooping abdominal muscles and tension-free neck.

2 Start with your legs at a 90-degree angle to your body and breathe in as you extend them only very slightly away from you. This is the first movement of a Rollover, where it is important that you develop abdominal control and not rely on your neck, back, legs and arms.

3 As you exhale, draw the legs back towards you. Emphasise your scooping abdominals and squeeze the ball gently and constantly for additional inside thigh work.

4 Repeat 5–6 times.

SPINAL MOBILITY & CONTROL

(continued)

ROLLOVERS

1 Begin as for Rollover Prep. Inhale as you extend your legs slightly away as a preparation for your next manoeuvre.

2 As you exhale, use your abdominals to lift your legs and hips up and over your head. Try to lengthen your waist up toward the ceiling and keep most of your weight on the back of your shoulders instead of compressing your neck.

3 Inhale to maintain your position, legs parallel to the floor—relax in your throat and draw your shoulders down.

4 As you exhale, roll down through your spine with control. Imagine lengthening between each spinal segment.

5 As you return to your neutral alignment, keep your abdominals scooping deeply.

6 Repeat 3–5 times.

SPINAL ROTATION

Purpose *To maintain a healthy range of motion throughout the spine and encourage muscular support during twisting movement. Pelvic and shoulder girdle stability are also a component of this exercise.*

SPINE TWIST

1 Start seated on your ball with your feet hip-width apart, or closer together to challenge your balance. Inhale, emphasising the length and strength of your abdominals and back. Extend your arms sideways at shoulder height, palms facing up and shoulders drawing down.

2 As you exhale, rotate your torso with a double pulse action without moving your hips or the ball. Try not to collapse the body—use your abdominals for movement control and think of everything from the waist up spiralling up toward the ceiling.

3 Breathe in as you return to face the front. Keep the ball glued to one spot on the floor and continue lengthening up out of the lower back and hips. Shoulders down at the top of this position.

4 Repeat and alternate sides, 8–10 times.

NOTE

Imagine your sitting bones are set in concrete despite the ball's movement and softness. Be buoyant, though stable and imagine creating a little more space between each vertebra.

GLUTEALS & ADDUCTORS

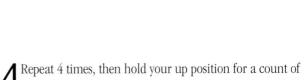

Purpose *To strengthen and tone the back of the hips and thighs for improved muscle balance. Strong hip, gluteal and inside thigh muscles (adductors) contribute to a stable pelvis and lower back. Abdominal control and core stability are also a strong feature because the ball creates an unstable foundation.*

BOTTOM LIFT SERIES

1 Prepare by sitting on the ball and walking forward so that you roll your pelvis under and lie on the ball. Continue walking until your head, neck and shoulders are fully supported and place your hands either under your head or on your hips. Ensure that your knee alignment is correct, with your kneecaps pointing forward and your knees not too far out over your toes. Heels should almost touch each other and toes should be slightly splayed.

2 Your focus should now remain on the muscles at the tops of the back of your thighs and the lower section of your buttocks (hamstrings and gluteals). Try to maintain a long sensation of your waist and thighs. Inhale as you lower your pelvis, without moving the ball.

3 Exhale, lift your pelvis using your hamstrings and gluteals without over-using your lower back. Think of stretching the fronts of your thighs upward and long.

4 Repeat 4 times, then hold your up position for a count of 10, maintaining a calm lateral breathing pattern.

5 After sustaining your Bottom Lift, proceed to squeeze the tops of your thighs together with small, quick pulses. Inhale for 4 pulses, exhale for 4 pulses. Repeat this breathing sequence as you continue to squeeze, 5–6 times. Maintain focus on the muscles of the lower part of your buttocks throughout.

GLUTEALS & ADDUCTORS

(continued)

SIDE BALANCE

1 Lie on your side with the ball between your ankles. Keep the legs slightly forward of your hips and lie directly on your side so that you can balance on your thighbone. Lengthen your legs away from you and focus on your abdominals—especially your underneath side, as that is what helps you gain balance.

2 Breathe in while you prepare your balance and press your abdominals firmly toward your spine.

3 As you exhale, squeeze your top leg into the ball and lengthen your waist.

4 Inhale as you release your squeeze on the ball, but don't let the abdominals go!

5 Repeat 10–12 times each side, ensuring your lower back doesn't arch or strain.

PROGRESSION

If you feel stable and strong through your abdominals and back, try squeezing both legs into the ball and lifting your underneath ankle from the floor. Remember to balance on your thighbone and focus on the underneath side of your waist muscles to maintain your stability. Repeat 5–6 times.

SCAPULA STABILITY & BACK STRENGTHENING

Purpose *To develop and strengthen the muscles of the middle and upper back for better posture. Increasing the endurance of these postural muscles will help alleviate neck and shoulder tension.*

ARM OPENINGS

1 Begin kneeling with the ball in front of you and against your thighs. Roll forward on the ball so your knees lift just off the floor and push the lower part of your ribcage gently into the ball so you can lift your chest bone slightly —this action will allow you better use of the postural muscles of your upper back, relieving stress from your neck. Keep your abdominals lifted and your shoulder blades drawing down flat against your ribcage throughout. Inhale to prepare.

2 As you exhale, raise your arms sideways without hitching your shoulders up or squeezing your shoulder blades. The idea of scapula stability is to move your shoulder joints without allowing your shoulder blades to move from their ideal anatomical alignment. Hold momentarily.

3 Lower your arms as you inhale.

4 Repeat 6–10 times.

PROGRESSION
Add hand weights of a kilo or half a kilo to challenge the stability of your back and shoulder girdle and gain further strength. The weight should not be so heavy that muscle strain occurs in the neck. Focus on the middle of your back bracing and keeping your abdominals lifted.

Scapula Stability & Back Strengthening

(continued)

Back Extension

1 Begin as for Arm Openings, though place your fingers under your forehead and drape yourself forward over the ball. Engage your abdominals and prepare yourself to keep the front of your torso stable against the ball.

2 Breathe in as you lift your upper torso—imagine bending from your mid-thoracic area. Ensure your abdominals remain lifted and your shoulders draw down.

3 Exhale as your lower yourself. Maintain the lift of your abdominals so that you're prepared and stable for the next repetition.

4 Repeat 6–10 times.

For further shoulder and upper back strengthening and postural endurance, extend your arms to a 'v' position at the top of the lift. Inhale, lift. Exhale, extend your arms—keep your shoulders down. Inhale, bring your hands back to your forehead. Exhale, lower.

FULL BODY INTEGRATION

Purpose *To ultimately challenge the individual's ability to have a true 'full body' focus, combining the need to stabilise the lower back with strong abdominal muscles, maintain a steady shoulder girdle position and to coordinate isolated movement of the limbs.*

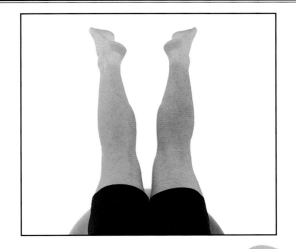
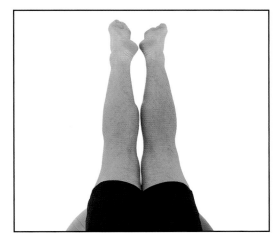

Leg Beats

1 Begin kneeling with the ball in front of you and roll forward so that your thighs and pelvis are on the ball. Support your weight by your hands or elbows and keep your shoulder blades flat against your ribs with your abdominals lifting, acting like a 'sling' to support your lower back. This upper body position must remain stable throughout.

2 Now, focus on a long waist and strong long legs. You may slightly turn your thighs out. Beat your legs together with small crisp sideways movements, from the tops of the back of your thighs, down to your heels. Inhale for 4 beats, exhale for 4 beats.

3 Repeat 6–10 times.

NOTE
If you are on your hands slightly soften your elbow joints so that they point backwards and keep your shoulders directly over your hands. Emphasise abdominals up, nose down and shoulder blades down and flat.

FULL BODY INTEGRATION

(continued)

NOTE
Keep in mind the parts of you that should remain strong and stable and the parts that are actually moving. Your elbows are the only parts that move —keep the rest of you long and buoyant.

Push-ups

1 Begin as for Leg Beats and walk forward only as far as you are able to maintain a stable back and shoulder girdle. Start with the ball under your thighs and walk your hands further away from the ball as you are able to progress your position. Hands under shoulders, shoulder blades flat, abdominals lifted and waist and thighs 'long'.

2 Inhale as you bend your elbows so they point backward. Shoulder blades should not squeeze together and lower back should not sag. Remember—nose down, abdominals up.

3 Exhale as you press up, pushing through the heels of your hands.

4 Repeat 6–10 times.

Stretch & Relax

Purpose _To release muscle and joint tension and achieve more suppleness and mobility. After exercising muscles it is beneficial to stretch them so that they maintain or gain length and are less susceptible to strain or injury. After stretching, your mind and body feel invigorated._

THORACIC PUSH THROUGH

1 Kneel with the ball in front of you and place both hands on top of the ball. Allow the ball to roll away so that your hips are directly over your knees. If this is too precarious simply sit on your feet.

2 Allow your chest to fall through your arms toward the floor. Take care with your shoulders—you may have to bend or straighten your elbows to adjust your position more comfortably. The idea is to gently mobilise and release your mid-thoracic spine, where a lot of postural tension builds up.

3 Breathe normally and relax for 5–6 full breaths. Repeat if necessary.

STRETCH & RELAX

(continued)

OVERHEAD REACH

1 Begin in a squat position with your feet apart for greater stability. Lean against the ball and roll back slightly. Reach your arms out in front of you.

2 Breathe in as you push backward into the ball, rolling backwards and reaching your arms up above your head as you arch your upper back over the top of the ball. You may or may not completely straighten your legs.

3 Exhale, circling your arms and bending your knees to resume your squat position.

4 Repeat 4–6 times. Keep your abdominals firm to stabilise your lower back against the ball and relax your upper back to allow for fluid movement.

NOTE

Upon returning from the back extension, 'chin to chest' first before continuing to bend your knees. If you require neck support, place your hands behind your head and neck and perhaps not extend quite as far backwards.

Stretch & Relax

(continued)

Hamstring Stretch

1 Start by sitting on the ball with your feet wider than hip-width apart for greater stability. Place your hands on your thighs.

2 Without moving your feet or your hands roll the ball backward to achieve a stretch for the backs of your legs. Breathe normally and gently hold your abdominals for back support. Hold for at least 20–30 seconds and repeat again.

Note
For an additional stretch lift your toes off the floor and flex your ankles.

Hip Flexor Stretch

1 Kneel on one knee with your other leg bent out in front of you and both hips squarely facing front. Lift your abdominals up toward your spine and tuck you tailbone under as though doing the 'pelvic tilt' exercise.

2 If you cannot feel a stretch at the front of your (kneeling) hip, then you may slightly lean forward without releasing your pelvic tuck. Lengthen your waist upward as you lean forward to protect your lower back from arching.

3 Hold for at least 30 seconds and repeat on the other leg.

GLOSSARY

ADDUCTORS
Muscles of the inner thighs, which draw the legs together.

GLUTEALS
Muscle group of the buttocks, which contribute to hip movement and stability of the pelvis and lumbar spine.

HAMSTRINGS
Muscle group of the back of the thigh, from the sitting bone to the back of the knee, which bends the knee or assists in backward leg motion.

HIP FLEXORS
Muscles at the front of the hip that lift the thigh toward the torso.

OBLIQUE ABDOMINALS
Muscles at the sides of the abdomen that predominantly twist, or rotate, the torso.

SCAPULA
The shoulder blade, which makes up part of the shoulder joint.

CONCLUSION

Pilates is a unique movement re-education system because it acknowledges the body as the integrated whole that it is, and aims for each individual to develop to their fitness potential.

The Pilates way of moving is a superior method of training muscles for greater endurance, both for postural benefit and dynamically. Core strengthening is becoming more widely practised and Pilates techniques have long been renowned for including this fundamental component in overall fitness training. In essence, the Pilates Method is built upon intuitive movement pathways.

This practice encourages optimal full-range movement of all joints, as well as improving the grace and efficiency with which the body moves.

The beauty of practising Pilates is that improvements in strength, stability and freer moving joints are achieved by persevering with a methodical and frequent approach to the work. Each time you begin your workout remember to apply yourself mentally—think logically about what you are doing, breathe in a regular manner and purposefully move your body. Be kind to your body and condition it with care—it has to last you a lifetime!

About the Authors

JENNIFER POHLMAN completed a Bachelor of Dance at the Victorian College of the Arts in Melbourne and has almost a decade of experience with the Pilates Method. She began Pilates training first as a dancer, as a rehabilitative measure for chronic lower back injury. The natural progression to instructor training happened by means of an apprentice-based course over an intensive six-month period. Following two years of teaching in busy Pilates studios and physiotherapy centres, both in Brisbane and on the Gold Coast, Jennifer established her own business 'Pilates InsideOut'. She began by freelancing throughout the Tweed and Gold Coast regions and now teaches the Method from her studio in Kirra on the Gold Coast.

RODNEY SEARLE has a background in various physical disciplines. Primarily a professional classical ballet dancer, he began Pilates nine years ago following ankle surgery while studying at the Australian Ballet School. Rodney has diversified his skills with many years of gymnastics, martial arts and various dance genres. He is a qualified instructor in the Pilates Method, having studied with Michael King (of Pilates Institute, U.K.) and instructor-trainers from Australia's Body Arts & Science, and enjoys teaching a wide range of clients on the Gold Coast. Rodney has found Pilates body conditioning to be an invaluable contribution to developing movement intelligence. His passion lies in training elite athletes and dancers.

SIMPLY
BALL & BAND

Art Director: Karen Moores
Editor: Rose Inserra
Design: Sam Gimmer, Katerine Power
Photography: Glenn Weiss

CONTENTS

Introduction 69

Points to Remember 71

Warm Up & Stability 72

Level 1 Workout 82
Introduction to Level 1 Workout 83
Level 1 Cardio Set A 84
Level 1 Strength Set A (chest) 85
Level 1 Cardio Set B 86
Level 1 Strength Set B (Back & Biceps) 87
Level 1 Cardio Set C 88
Level 1 Strength Set C (Legs) 89
Level 1 Cardio Set D 90
Level 1 Strength Set D (Abdominals) 91
Level 1 Cardio Set E 92
Level 1 Strength Set E (Triceps) 93

Level 2 Workout 94
Introduction to Level 2 Workout 95
Level 2 Cardio Set A 96
Level 2 Strength Set A (chest) 97
Level 2 Cardio Set B 98
Level 2 Strength Set B (Back & Biceps) 99
Level 2 Cardio Set C 100
Level 2 Strength Set C (Legs) 101
Level 2 Cardio Set D 102
Level 2 Strength Set D (Abdominals) 103
Level 2 Cardio Set E 104
Level 2 Strength Set E (Triceps) 105

Level 3 Workout 106
Introduction to Level 3 Workout 107
Level 3 Cardio Set A 108
Level 3 Strength Set A (chest) 109
Level 3 Cardio Set B 110
Level 3 Strength Set B (Back & Biceps) 111
Level 3 Cardio Set C 112
Level 3 Strength Set C (Legs) 113
Level 3 Cardio Set D 114
Level 3 Strength Set D (Abdominals) 115
Level 3 Cardio Set E 116
Level 3 Strength Set E (Triceps) 117

Cool Down & Stretch 118

Conclusion 125

Glossary 126

About the Author 128

INTRODUCTION

Hi and welcome to *Simply Ball & Band*. This book is your guide and reference to your new fitball and resistance band workout DVD. Simply Ball & Band is presented to you by Dina Matty from *Pilates the Authentic Way* and Mark Richardson who brought you *Fighting Fit*. It is a progressive workout that has 3 classes with 3 respective levels combining a focus on strength, core stability and cardiovascular fitness.

If you have never used this equipment before, do not worry, because the class is suitable for a complete beginner who is interested in enjoying the benefits of the fitball and resistance band. Experienced fitball users are offered loads of fun and strong challenges in the advanced levels.

Simply Ball & Band keeps you
• trim with a progressive aerobic component
• toned with a gradual strength program
• happy because it enables you to have fun with the equipment provided in the comfort of your own home with the proper instruction that will see you achieving results.

Using *Simply Ball & Band* is an easy way to exercise but still includes all the major components of any professional fitness and strength program offering a beginner level through to advanced so that you can progress at your own pace. It begins with a comprehensive warm up and flexibility component and finishes with a calm, relaxing cool down.

POINTS TO REMEMBER

CORE BRACING & POSTURE

Today everyone is out to achieve maximum 'core stability'. But what is core stability and how do we strengthen our core? The core is made up of a number of different muscles located in the centre or trunk of your body and the lower back and hip. Your centre muscles include the rectus abdominus, transverse abdominus and obliques. Your lower back and hip are comprised of the gluteus medius, gluteus maximus and the adductors (inner thighs). To ensure that all strength and even cardio exercises are executed safely to prevent injury, it is important to brace and strengthen your core. This is achieved by engaging your centre muscles by drawing your tummy in and up under your ribs, or imagine your navel being pulled in toward your spine and up under your rib cage.

With certain exercises (mostly when your legs are straight) you can also engage your hip and lower back (centre muscles are also included in the lower back), by squeezing your glutes and your adductors (inner thighs). Furthermore, most exercises require a set posture in the shoulders and upper back in order to prevent injury in the upper torso. This is achieved by dropping your shoulders down and drawing your shoulder blades together. Remember, since we are all aiming for peak health and fitness, it would be unfortunate to cause an injury whilst striving to do just that, hence the importance of your core bracing and posture.

BREATHING & FOCUS

It is common for people to hold their breath during, or when executing any exercise, particularly when doing strength exercises. It is important to breathe during all your exercises, and it is most beneficial to emphasise your exhalation in time with the exertion part of the exercise to help you focus on technique and core bracing. For example, when doing push ups inhale as you lower down and exhale to push up.

CONTRAINDICATIONS

Because of the physical nature of the fitball and flexiband workout program it is advisable that you obtain permission from your family medical practitioner if you have any past or present injuries or concerns that are listed below:

- pregnancy
- high/low blood pressure
- heart disease
- joint injuries - back, neck, shoulder, elbow, wrist, hip, knee and ankle
- muscular injuries
- diabetes

Although designed for everyone, some people may be limited by personal conditions (listed above) when performing some of these exercises. For this reason and for variety, we have included variations of exercises targeting specific muscle groups.

Warm Up & Stability

The purpose of the warm up and stability is to stretch your body for the work out ahead, familiarise yourself with the ball, and to check correct postural technique, so you can get the most benefit from your workout, whilst preventing any injuries.

Breathing

1 Lie on your back, legs elevated on the ball, arms by your side and palms to the floor. Draw shoulder blades down and back, keeping your neck nice and long.

2 Inhale and expand your back on the mat. Exhale and draw the core muscles in and up (core muscles include transverse abdominus, obliques and rectus).

3 Inhale for three or four counts, then exhale for three or four counts.

4 Repeat twice more.

Spinal Rotation

1 From previous position raise arms horizontal, palms down to the floor.

2 Inhale and roll the ball to one side, going as far as you can whilst keeping both shoulder blades drawn down and on the floor.

3 Exhale, draw core muscles in and up to return to centre.

4 Repeat for three counts on each side.

Hip Stretch

1 From the previous position roll the ball away from you and cross the right ankle onto the left knee. Hold under the knee with both hands, reaching the left hand around the side and the right in between the legs, pressing the right knee open to feel the stretch in the hip.

2 Inhale to prepare, exhale as you stretch and press the knee away and stretch the hip.

3 Hold the stretch for three or four counts.

4 Repeat on other side.

Spinal Massage

1 From previous position, pick the ball up with your feet and pass the ball to your hands. Keep your legs in table-top position (knees over your hips, shins horizontal).

2 Draw your core muscles in and up.

3 Draw your chin to your chest, gently rocking forward and back three to five times, massaging the spine.

4 On your final rock forward sit up, crossing your legs.

Core Flexion

1 Place both feet on the ball, draw the ball into the back of your legs and place your fingertips lightly on the back of your head (don't pull on your neck).

2 Inhale, curl up and forward, hold for two counts then release back down.

3 Inhale to prepare and exhale as you hold, drawing the core muscles in and up.

4 Repeat four more times.

WARM UP & STABILITY

(continued)

LOWER BACK & HIP STRETCH

1 From the previous position (legs crossed), roll the ball forward walking your hands down the ball, draw your chin to your chest.

2 Inhale, extending from the lower back. Exhale while gently folding forward.

3 Hold for three or four counts.

4 Roll the ball slowly back to the original position.

HAMSTRING & INNER THIGH STRETCH

1 Extend both legs to the side, point knees and toes to the ceiling.

2 Walk the ball forward gently, stretching the hamstring and adductor (inner thigh) muscles.

3 Inhale, drawing your core muscles in and up, exhale and stretch.

4 Hold the stretch for three to four counts and walk the ball back to the original position.

5 Repeat Lower Back & Hip Stretch on the other side.

BACK STRETCH

1 Come up onto your knees, sit your hips back onto your heels, walk the ball forward so that your back is flat and you feel the stretch in your back and sides of your torso.

2 Draw your core muscles in and up as you move forward.

3 Inhale to prepare and exhale as you walk the ball forward into the stretch.

4 Hold the stretch for three to four counts.

HORIZONTAL SIDE STRETCH

1 From the previous position, keep the hips back on the heels, roll the ball to one side, walking the hands over the ball so you can feel the stretch in the lats (the muscle by your ribs).

2 Inhale as you walk over and exhale as you stretch.

3 Draw your core muscles in and up as you hold the stretch for three to four counts.

4 Repeat on the other side.

CAT CURL STRETCH

1 Walk the ball back to the centre, raise your hips off your heels, walk out to a flat back position.

2 Inhale to prepare, exhale pulling up into the Cat Curl Stretch.

3 Draw your core muscles in and up to feel the stretch across the middle of your back.

4 Hold the stretch for three to four counts.

PRONE STABILITY

1 Walk the ball back in, lay your stomach over the ball and place your hands in front of you. Roll forward on the ball, extend the legs and keep your toes on the floor, keeping your shoulders down and back.

2 Return to the start position, walk forward to the hips. This time raise legs in the air and draw core muscles in and up.

3 Return to the start position, walk forward to the thigh and hold for three to four counts.

4 Repeat step 3.

WARM UP & STABILITY

(continued)

HIP FLEXOR, CALF & ACHILLES STRETCH

1 Roll the ball to one side, place your hand on the ball and step the opposite leg forward with your knee in line with your ankle. Keep your back knee on the floor to stretch your hip flexor.

2 Draw your core muscles in and up to stay out of your back.

3 Hold for three to four counts.

4 Lift your back knee off the floor, sinking your hips low to the floor to increase the stretch. Hold for three to four counts.

5 Lift your weight, draw the back foot forward and place your heel down. Keep your weight forward and stretch your calf and achilles. Hold for three to four counts.

6 Bring feet together, roll the ball to the other side and repeat Hip Flexor, Calf & Achilles Stretch on the other side.

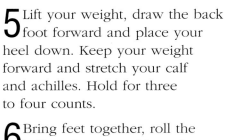
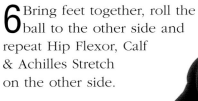

CORE ROTATION

1 Stand up, feet hip-width apart and ball at hip height. With your ball, turn to one side transferring your weight onto that foot, twisting your core and looking over your shoulder. Repeat on the other side, then repeat this at chest then shoulder heights and return back down to the hips.

2 Draw core muscles in and up, keeping your hips square to the front. Rotate from the waist during the whole exercise.

3 Place the ball on the floor, walk around to the front and sit on the ball.

WARM UP & STABILITY

(continued)

IMPRINTING & LEG EXTENSION

1 Sit tall on your ball, drawing your core muscles in and up, with your shoulders back and hands by your side. Maintain this posture and lift one heel off the floor. Hold for one count and repeat on the other side.

2 Maintain the above position and lift your whole foot off the floor, staying tall and keeping balance. Hold for one count then repeat on the other side.

3 Keep the previous posture, raise your foot off the floor and flex your leg upward at the knee, staying tall and keeping balance. Hold for two counts and repeat on the other side.

BRIDGING

1 Maintaining the above position, draw your core muscles in and up, and walk forward so your lower back is on the ball. Hold for two counts, then walk back to the original position, keeping your shoulders forward over your hips.

2 Repeat again so that your shoulder blades reach the ball. Hold for two counts and return to the original position.

3 Repeat again so that your head and shoulders are on the ball in full bridge position, keep your hips lifted by squeezing your glutes. Hold for three to four counts and return to the original position.

4 Repeat step three.

Single Hamstring Stretch

1 Sit tall on your ball, extending one leg forward with your heel on the floor and your toes pointing to the ceiling.

2 Inhale, drawing your core muscles in and up. Exhale and lean forward, maintaining a long spine. Stretch the hamstring.

3 Hold the stretch for three to four counts.

4 Repeat on the other leg.

Double Hamstring Stretch

1 Sit tall on your ball.

2 Draw your core muscles in and up, extend your knees, rolling the ball back. Lean forward, sliding your hands down your legs.

3 Inhale to prepare, and exhale using your hands to pull yourself gently toward your legs.

4 Hold for three to four counts.

5 Draw your core muscles in and up as you roll your spine back to the original position.

WARM UP & STABILITY

(continued)

SIDE STRETCH

1 Sit tall on your ball with your feet wide, place one elbow on your thigh.

2 Draw your core muscles in and up.

3 Inhale and lift your opposite arm up to your ear. While exhaling, increase the stretch over to the side.

4 Hold for three to four counts.

SIDE & LAT STRETCH

1 From the last position, twist forward, reaching your opposite arm, palm to the front.

2 Hold for three to four counts.

Neck Stretch

1 From the last position, draw your core muscles in and up to pull yourself into a seated position. Sit tall.

2 Inhale as you place your resting hand behind your back and your opposite hand over your head. Exhale and gently pull your ear to your shoulder, stretching your neck.

3 Hold for three to four counts.

4 Repeat the Side Stretch, Side & Lat Stretch, and then the Neck Stretch on the other side.

LEVEL 1 WORKOUT

CARDIO SET A

STRENGTH SET A (CHEST)

THIGH PUSH UP
BRIDGING CHEST PRESS

CARDIO SET B

STRENGTH SET B (BACK & BICEPS)

PRONE BACK EXTENSION
SEATED ROW

CARDIO SET C

STRENGTH SET C (LEGS)

SQUAT
WALL SQUAT

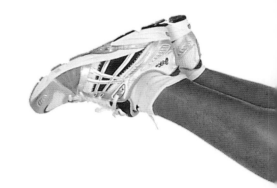

CARDIO SET D

STRENGTH SET D (ABDOMINALS)

ASSISTED SINGLE LEG LOWER & LIFT
ASSISTED CORE FLEXION

CARDIO SET E

STRENGTH SET E (TRICEPS)

OVERHEAD TRICEP EXTENSION WITH BAND
OVERHEAD TRICEP EXTENSION WITH BALL

INTRODUCTION TO LEVEL 1 WORKOUT

CARDIO

The exercises in this level are performed predominantly seated on the ball, offering a low impact cardiovascular workout. It is important to be aware of your posture, pulling your core muscles in and up for good alignment and balance. Your aim is to be confidently centred on the ball for all the exercises at this level whilst aiming to keep the same speed as your instructors on the DVD. Once you have achieved this, move on to level 2 cardio.

STRENGTH

The exercises in this level develop a strong foundation in your basic core strength. The emphasis at this level is to be aware of your core muscles, drawing them inward and upward, and drawing your shoulders down and back. Squeeze your glutes and inner thighs when appropriate. Additionally, you should be aiming to complete eight to ten reps of all the exercises, with a 1-2-1 tempo. The tempo applies to the length of time of (1) the initial movement, (2) the holding position and (3) the return to the original position, respectively. When you have reached this goal with strong core strength, good technique and the correct tempo, challenge yourself further and move onto the next level.

LEVEL 1 CARDIO SET A

BOUNCING	x 8
SIDE TAP	x 8
BOUNCING	x 8
SIDE TAP	x 8
STAR JUMP	x 8
BOUNCING	x 8
SIDE TAP	x 8
STAR JUMP	x 8

Bouncing

Side Tap

Star Jump

Level 1 Strength
Set A - Chest

Thigh Push Up

1 Squat behind the ball, roll forward so your thighs are over the ball, shoulders over and in line with the wrists, palms on the floor.

2 Draw your core muscles in and up with shoulders down and back. Squeeze your glutes and inner thighs.

3 Inhale, bend your elbows to the side and lower your chest to the floor. Exhale and push up. Return to the original position.

4 Lower for one count, hold the position for two counts and push up for one count.

Bridging Chest Press

1 Sitting tall on your ball, walk out to the full bridge position, place your hands up and together above your shoulders.

2 Keeping your neck long and your shoulders down, draw your core muscles in and up and squeeze your glutes and inner thighs to keep your hips raised.

3 Picture a triangle where your hands are at the top point, inhaling as you lower your hands to the lower points of the triangle. Exhale and push your hands to the top.

4 With your own resistance or tension, lower yourself down for one count, hold for two counts, and push back up for one count.

Level 1 Cardio Set B

Bouncing	x 8
Side Tap	x 8
Star Jump	x 8
Bouncing add Reach & Pull	x 8
Side Tap add Jab	x 8
Star Jump add Shoulder Press	x 8
Bouncing with Reach & Pull	x 8
Side Tap with Jab	x 8
Star Jump with Shoulder Press	x 8

Bouncing

Side Tap

Star Jump

Bouncing add
Reach & Pull

Side Tap
add Jab

Star Jump add Shoulder Press

Level 1 Strength
Set B - Back & Biceps

Prone Back Extension

1 Squat behind the ball and roll forward. Your hips should be on the ball with your legs extended and your toes tucked under and touching the floor. Place your fingertips on the back of your head and fold forward.

2 Squeeze your glutes and pull in and up with your core muscles.

3 Inhale to prepare, exhale as you extend at the hip, raising your upper body to a prone position above the floor.

4 Lift for one count, hold for two counts and lower in one count.

Seated Row

1 Sitting tall on the ball, place both feet over the middle of your band. Wrap the ends around your hands, reaching your arms' length.

2 Draw the core muscles in and up.

3 Inhale to prepare, exhale and pull the band, drawing your elbows just past your ribs. Squeeze your shoulder blade to open up your chest.

4 Pull back for one count, hold for two counts and release for one count.

LEVEL 1 CARDIO SET C

BOUNCING WITH REACH & PULL	x 8
SIDE TAP WITH JAB	x 8
STAR JUMP WITH SHOULDER PRESS	x 8
SQUAT & LIFT	x 4
SQUAT & LIFT (DOUBLE TIME)	x 8
SQUAT & LIFT	x 4
SQUAT & LIFT (DOUBLE TIME)	x 8

Bouncing with
Reach & Pull

Star Jump with
Shoulder Press

Side Tap with Jab

Squat & Lift

LEVEL 1 STRENGTH
SET C - LEGS

SQUAT

1 Stand with your feet parallel and hip width apart, sit your hips back so your weight is over your heels.

2 As you inhale, squat down aiming to lower your hips level with your knees so you can just see your toes over your knees. Hold while drawing the core muscles in and up.

3 Exhale as you push up from your heels, squeezing your glutes to a standing position.

4 Lower for one count. Hold the squat for two counts and push up for one count.

WALL SQUAT

1 Place the ball on the wall and lean the curve of your back against the ball. Position your feet parallel and hip width apart, and sit your hips back so that your weight is over your heels.

2 Inhale to lower, supporting your lower back at all times with the ball, aiming to keep your hips in line with your knees so you can just see your toes over your knees.

3 Exhale as you push up from your heels, squeezing your glutes to a standing position.

4 Lower for one count. Hold the squat for two counts and push up for one count.

LEVEL 1 CARDIO SET D

BOUNCING WITH REACH & PULL	x 8
SIDE TAP WITH JAB	x 8
STAR JUMP WITH SHOULDER PRESS	x 8
SQUAT & LIFT (DOUBLE TIME)	x 8
(WALK AROUND BALL TO) SQUAT TAP	x 3
(WALK BALL THROUGH LEGS AND SIT)	
SQUAT & LIFT (DOUBLE TIME)	x 8
(WALK AROUND BALL TO) SQUAT TAP	x 3
(WALK BALL THROUGH LEGS AND SIT)	

Bouncing with Reach & Pull

Side Tap with Jab

Star Jump with Shoulder Press

Squat & Lift

Squat & Tap

LEVEL 1 STRENGTH SET D - ABDOMINALS

ASSISTED SINGLE LEG LOWER LIFT

1 Lie on the floor with your legs over the ball so that your calves and thighs are in contact with the ball. Place your arms by your sides, palms down.

2 Draw your core muscles in and up so your lower back is on the floor.

3 Inhale as you lower your heel to the floor keeping your knee bent, and exhale as you draw your core muscles in raising your leg back to the ball.

4 Lower your leg for one count, hold for two counts and lift for one count.

ASSISTED CORE FLEXION

1 Lie on the band so your band is aligned with your spine. Place your legs over the ball making sure that calves and thighs are in contact with the ball.

2 Hold your band at the outside edges, pulling on the band to create a nice strong tension. Keep your elbow open so as not to pull on your neck.

3 Inhale to prepare, curl your head and shoulders forward. Exhale and draw your core muscles in and up, then release down to the floor.

4 Lift for one count, hold for two counts and release to the floor in one.

LEVEL 1 CARDIO SET E

BOUNCING WITH REACH & PULL	x 8
SIDE TAP WITH JAB	x 8
STAR JUMP WITH SHOULDER PRESS	x 8
SQUAT & LIFT (DOUBLE TIME)	x 8
(WALK AROUND BALL TO) SQUAT TAP	x 3
(WALK BALL THROUGH LEGS AND SIT)	
SQUAT & LIFT (DOUBLE TIME)	x 8
(WALK AROUND BALL TO) SQUAT TAP	x 3
(WALK BALL THROUGH LEGS AND SIT)	

Bouncing with
Reach & Pull

Side Tap with Jab

Star Jump with
Shoulder Press

Squat & Lift

Squat & Tap

Walk Ball through Legs & Sit

Level 1 Strength
Set E - Triceps

Overhead Tricep Extension with Band

1 Sit tall on the band on your ball. With feet hip width apart, hold your band at the outside edges and pull on the band. This will create a nice strong tension.

2 Pull your core muscles in and up, keeping your elbows close to your head.

3 Inhale to prepare, and exhale as you raise your hands above your head, extending your elbows. Flex your triceps.

4 Raise for one count, hold the extension for two counts, and release for one count.

Overhead Tricep Extension with Ball

1 Stand in a comfortable position and hold your ball with your arms extended over your head.

2 Keep your weight forward onto the balls of your feet, drawing your core muscles in and up.

3 Inhale to lower the ball down to the back of your head, keeping your elbow close to your head. Exhale while raising the ball and extending at the elbows. Flex your triceps.

4 Lower in one count, hold for two counts, and extend for one count.

Level 2 Workout

Cardio Set A

Strength Set A (Chest)

Bridging Chest Press with Band
Shin Push Up

Cardio Set B

Strength Set B (Back & Biceps)

Seated Row with Leg Extension
Prone Back Extension with Lat Pulldown

Cardio Set C

Strength Set C (Legs)

Wall Lunge
Lunge with Shoulder Press

Cardio Set D

Strength Set D (Abdominals)

Ball in Hands Core Flexion
Double Leg Lower & Lift

Cardio Set E

Strength Set E (Triceps)

Prone Tricep Extension
Prone Tricep Extension with Band

INTRODUCTION TO LEVEL 2 WORKOUT

CARDIO

The exercises in this level are performed standing up, using the ball to increase the intensity. This low impact cardiovascular workout utilises dynamic footwork, longer levers and a more complex choreography. It is important to be aware of your posture, pulling your core muscles in and up for good alignment and balance. Your aim is to be able to confidently perform all the exercises at this level whilst aiming to keep the same speed as your instructors on the DVD. For an extra challenge try performing all the level 2 cardio blocks in a row, just by queuing forward on your DVD. Then try level 3 cardio.

STRENGTH

Level 2 strength still focuses on core strength whilst progressing the exercises to an intermediate level with more balance and stability control, therefore promoting increased strength. At this level you should be aiming to complete eight to ten reps of all the exercises, with a 1-3-1 tempo. When you have reached this goal with strong core strength, good technique and the correct tempo, challenge yourself further and move onto the next level.

LEVEL 2 CARDIO SET A

WALK FORWARD TAP	x 2
WALK FORWARD KNEE	x 2
SIDE TAP	x 8
WALK FORWARD KNEE add SHOULDER PRESS	x 2
SIDE TAP add CHEST PRESS	x 8
WALK FORWARD KNEE with SHOULDER PRESS	x 2
SIDE TAP with CHEST PRESS	x 8

Walk Forward Tap

Walk Forward Knee

Walk Forward Knee add Shoulder Press

Side Tap with Chest Press

Side Tap

LEVEL 2 STRENGTH SET A - CHEST

BRIDGING CHEST PRESS WITH BAND

1 Sitting tall on your ball, place the band on the floor in front of the ball. Hold each end of the band and walk out to the full bridge position so that the ball is over the band. Place your hands up and together above your shoulders.

2 Keeping your neck long and your shoulders down, draw your core muscles in and up and squeeze your glutes and inner thighs to keep your hips raised.

3 Picture a triangle where your hands are at the top point. Inhale as you lower your hands to the lower points of the triangle and exhale while pushing your hands to the top using the resistance of the band.

4 Lowering down for one count, hold for three counts. Then push back up for one count.

SHIN PUSH UP

1 Squat behind the ball and roll forward so that your shins are over the ball, your shoulders over and in line with the wrists, palms on the floor.

2 Draw your core muscles in and up with shoulders down and back, squeeze your glutes and inner thighs.

3 Inhale, bend your elbows to the side and lower your chest to the floor. Exhale, push up and return to the original position.

4 Lower for one count, hold the position for three counts and push up for one count.

Level 2 Cardio Set B

Walk Forward Knee with Shoulder Press	x 2
Side Tap with Chest Press	x 8
Step Touch	x 8
Double Step Touch	x 4
Step Touch add Bounce	x 8
Double Step Touch add Full Circle	x 4
Step Touch with Bounce	x 8
Double Step Touch with Full Circle	x 4

Walk Forward Knee with Shoulder Press

Side Tap with Chest Press

Step Touch with Bounce

Double Step Touch with Full Circle

LEVEL 2 STRENGTH
SET B - BACK & BICEPS

SEATED ROW WITH LEG EXTENSION

1 Sitting tall on the ball, placing both feet over the middle of your band, wrap the ends around your hands. Lift one foot up and extend leg at the knee joint for the leg extension.

2 Draw the core muscles in and up.

3 Inhale to prepare, exhale and pull using the resistance of the band, drawing your elbows just past your ribs. Squeeze your shoulder blade to open up your chest. Aim for five repetitions, then repeat on the opposite leg.

4 Pull back for one count, hold for three counts and release for one count.

PRONE BACK EXTENSION WITH LAT PULLDOWN

1 Squat behind the ball and roll forward. Your hips should be on the ball with your legs extended and your toes tucked under and touching the floor. Place your fingertips on the back of your head and fold forward.

2 Squeeze your glutes and pull in and up with your core muscles.

3 Inhale to prepare, exhale as you extend at the hip, raising your upper body to a prone position over the floor. Inhale and reach your arms forward, then exhale and draw your elbows into the ribs, squeezing your lats and upper back. Inhale and place your fingertips behind your head and exhale as you lower yourself down.

4 Lift for one count, extend and flex the arms for three counts, and lower in one count.

LEVEL 2 CARDIO SET C

WALK FORWARD KNEE WITH SHOULDER PRESS	x 2
SIDE TAP WITH CHEST PRESS	x 8
STEP TOUCH WITH BOUNCE	x 8
DOUBLE STEP TOUCH WITH FULL CIRCLE	x 4
STEP TOUCH WITH BOUNCE	x 8
DOUBLE STEP TOUCH WITH FULL CIRCLE ADD SKIP	x 4
STEP TOUCH WITH BOUNCE	x 8
DOUBLE STEP TOUCH WITH FULL CIRCLE & SKIP	x 4

Side Tap with Chest Press

Walk Forward Knee
with Shoulder Press

Step Touch with Bounce

Double Step Touch with Full Circle

LEVEL 2 STRENGTH SET C - LEGS

WALL LUNGE

1 Place the ball on the wall and lean the curve of your back against the ball. Position your feet one foot forward and one foot back, hip-width apart. Make sure that your weight is centred over your front heel.

2 Inhale as you lower your body, supporting your lower back at all times with the ball. Aim to keep your hips in line with your knee so you can just see your toes over your knee.

3 Exhale while pushing up from your heel to standing position.

4 Lower for one count, hold the lunge for three counts, and push up for one count then repeat on the other leg.

LUNGE WITH SHOULDER PRESS

1 Stand with your feet parallel and hip-width apart. Sit your hips in a backward position so that your weight is over your heels, holding your ball at chest level.

2 As you inhale, squat down aiming to lower your hips level with your knees so that you can just see your toes over your knees. Hold, drawing the core muscles in and up and reach the ball over your head.

3 Exhale while pushing up from your heels, squeezing your glutes to a standing position and lowering the ball to the chest.

4 Lower for one count, hold the squat for three counts, and push up for one count then repeat on the other leg.

Level 2 Cardio Set D

WALK FORWARD KNEE WITH SHOULDER PRESS	x 2
SIDE TAP WITH CHEST PRESS	x 8
STEP TOUCH WITH BOUNCE	x 8
DOUBLE STEP TOUCH WITH FULL CIRCLE & SKIP	x 4
SQUAT & LIFT	x 4
SQUAT & KNEE	x 4

Walk Forward Knee
with Shoulder Press

Side Tap with
Chest Press

Step Touch with Bounce

Double Step Touch
with Full Circle & Skip

Squat and Knee

LEVEL 2 STRENGTH
SET D - ABDOMINALS

BALL IN HANDS CORE FLEXION

1 Lie on your back, ball in hands reaching to the ceiling and legs in table-top position.

2 Inhale while curling up and forward, reaching the ball towards your shins.

3 Exhale and hold, drawing core muscles in and up, and release. Make sure that your back does not arch off the floor.

4 Lift for one count, hold for three counts, and release to the floor in one.

DOUBLE LEG LOWER LIFT

1 Lie on the floor, ball in hands reaching to the ceiling and legs in table-top position.

2 Draw your core muscles in and up so that your lower back is not arching off the floor.

3 Inhale as you lower your heel(s) to the floor keeping your knee(s) bent. Exhale as you draw your core muscles in, raising your leg back to the table-top position. Repeat, alternating legs for four reps then add the double leg for two reps for a harder variation.

4 Lower your leg(s) for one count, hold for three counts and lift for one count.

LEVEL 2 CARDIO SET E

WALK FORWARD KNEE WITH SHOULDER PRESS	x 2
SIDE TAP WITH CHEST PRESS	x 8
STEP TOUCH WITH BOUNCE	x 8
DOUBLE STEP TOUCH WITH FULL CIRCLE & SKIP	x 4
SQUAT & KNEE	x 4

Walk Forward Knee
with Shoulder Press

Side Tap with
Chest Press

Step Touch with Bounce

Double Step Touch
with Full Circle & Skip

Squat and Knee

LEVEL 2 STRENGTH SET E - TRICEPS

PRONE TRICEP EXTENSION

1 Squat behind the ball and roll forward. Your hips should be on the ball with your legs extended and your toes tucked under and touching the floor. Pull your elbows just past your ribs, holding your fists at chest height.

2 Pull your core muscles in and up, keeping your elbows close to the sides of your body. Extend your elbows, reaching your arms back, so that your hands are above hip level.

3 Inhale to prepare, and exhale as you extend your elbows.

4 Extend for one count, hold the extension for three counts, and release for one count.

PRONE TRICEP EXTENSION WITH BAND

1 Squat behind the ball, placing the band in front of the ball on the floor. Roll forward and hold the ends of the band. Your hips should be on the ball with your legs extended and your toes tucked under and touching the floor. Pull your elbows just past your ribs, holding your fists at chest height.

2 Pull your core muscles in and up, keeping your elbows close to the sides of your body. Extend your elbows using the resistance of the band, reaching your arms back, so that your hands are above hip level.

3 Inhale to prepare, and exhale as you extend your elbows.

4 Extend for one count, hold the extension for three counts, and release for one count.

LEVEL 3 WORKOUT

CARDIO SET A

STRENGTH SET A (CHEST)

Hands on the Ball Push Up
Single Leg Push Up

CARDIO SET B

STRENGTH SET B (BACK & BICEPS)

Bent Over Row with Band
Prone Back Extension with Twist (Mega)

CARDIO SET C

STRENGTH SET C (LEGS)

Lunge on the Ball
Squat Hold with Shoulder Press

CARDIO SET D

STRENGTH SET D (ABDOMINALS)

Core Flexion with Double Leg Lower & Lift
Overhead Reach with Double Leg Stretch

CARDIO SET E

STRENGTH SET E (TRICEPS)

Wall Dips
Unassisted Dips

INTRODUCTION TO LEVEL 3 WORKOUT

CARDIO

Level 3 cardio is a progressive workout that
starts to build upon itself. Exercises from
both previous levels have been utilised, creating
an intricate workout using seated and standing
movements that you will already have confidence
in doing. This level will challenge you physically
and mentally, integrating dynamic footwork,
longer levers and complex choreography.
It is important to be aware of your posture,
pulling your core muscles in and up for good
alignment and balance. Your aim is to be able
to confidently perform all the exercises at this
level whilst aiming to keep the same speed
as your instructors on the DVD. For an extra
challenge try performing all the level 3 cardio
blocks in a row, just by queuing forward
on your DVD.

STRENGTH

At this stage you will have a strong foundation
in your core strength. This will allow you
to progress to where you will be challenged
technically at many levels. These exercises involve
emphasis in posture, balance, control, strength
and endurance. You should be aiming to complete
eight to ten reps of all the exercises, with a 2-3-2
tempo, strong core strength and good technique.
If you are confident in performing level 3 strength
in this format, try performing all the strength
together without the interruption
of the cardio workouts,
by queuing your
DVD forward.

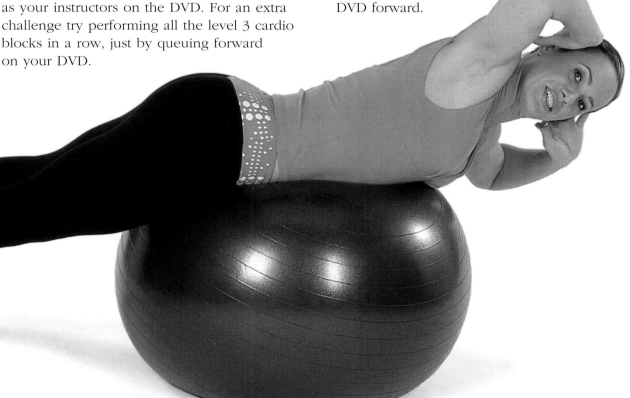

LEVEL 3 CARDIO SET A

BOUNCING WITH REACH & PULL	x 8
SIDE TAP WITH JAB	x 8
STAR JUMP WITH SHOULDER PRESS	x 8
SQUAT & LIFT (DOUBLE TIME)	x 8
(WALK AROUND BALL TO) SQUAT TAP	x 3
(WALK BALL THROUGH LEGS AND SIT)	
SQUAT & LIFT (DOUBLE TIME)	x 8
(WALK AROUND BALL TO) SQUAT TAP	x 3
(WALK BALL THROUGH LEGS AND SIT)	

Bouncing with
Reach & Pull

Side Tap with Jab

Star Jump with
Shoulder Press

Squat & Lift

Squat & Tap

Walk Ball through Legs & Sit

LEVEL 3 STRENGTH SET A - CHEST

HANDS ON BALL PUSH UP

1 Place your hands on the ball and walk your feet back into the push up position.

2 Draw your core muscles in and up with shoulders down and back. Squeeze your glutes and inner thighs.

3 Inhale, bend your elbows to the side and lower your chest to the ball. Exhale as you push up and return to the original position.

4 Lower for two counts, hold the position for three counts and push up for two counts.

SINGLE LEG PUSH UP

1 Squat behind the ball, rolling forward so that your shins are over the ball, shoulders over and in line with the wrists, palms on the floor.

2 Draw your core muscles in and up, shoulders down and back. Squeeze your glutes and inner thighs, raising one leg off the ball.

3 Inhale, bend your elbows to the side and lower your chest to the floor. Exhale and push up. Return to the original position.

4 Lower for two counts, hold the position for three counts and push up for two counts.

LEVEL 3 CARDIO SET B

WALK FORWARD KNEE WITH SHOULDER PRESS	x 2
SIDE TAP WITH CHEST PRESS	x 8
STEP TOUCH WITH BOUNCE	x 8
DOUBLE STEP TOUCH WITH FULL CIRCLE & SKIP	x 4
SQUAT & KNEE	x 4

Walk Forward Knee
with Shoulder Press

Side Tap with
Chest Press

Step Touch with Bounce

Double Step Touch
with Full Circle & Skip

Squat and Knee

LEVEL 3 STRENGTH
SET B - BACK & BICEPS

BENT OVER ROW WITH BAND

1 Stand behind the ball, placing one foot over the middle of the band. Wrap the ends of the band around your opposite hand and place the other on the ball.

2 Lean forward, drawing your core muscles in and up in flat back position, with one foot forward and the other foot back.

3 Inhale to prepare, exhale to pull your elbow up just past the ribs, and hand to the chest level, using the resistance of the band.

4 Pull for two counts, hold for three, and release for two counts.

PRONE BACK EXTENSION WITH TWIST (MEGA)

1 Squat behind the ball and roll forward. Your hips should be on the ball with your legs extended and your toes tucked under and touching the floor. Place your fingertips on the back of your head and fold forward.

2 Squeeze your glutes and pull in and up with your core muscles.

3 Inhale to prepare, exhale as you extend at the hip, raising your upper body to a prone position over the floor. Inhale and reach your arms forward. Exhale and draw your elbows into the ribs, squeezing your lats and upper back. Inhale and place your fingertips behind your head and exhale, twisting at the waist and aiming your elbow to the ceiling. Keep your chest and shoulders open at all times.

4 Lift for two count, extend and flex the arms and twist for three, and lower in two counts.

LEVEL 3 CARDIO SET C

BOUNCING WITH REACH & PULL	x 8
SIDE TAP WITH JAB	x 8
STAR JUMP WITH SHOULDER PRESS	x 8
SQUAT & LIFT (DOUBLE TIME)	x 8
(WALK AROUND BALL TO) SQUAT TAP	x 3
(WALK BALL THROUGH LEGS AND SIT)	
SQUAT & LIFT (DOUBLE TIME)	x 8
(WALK AROUND BALL TO) SQUAT TAP	x 3
(WALK BALL THROUGH LEGS AND SIT)	

Bouncing with
Reach & Pull

Side Tap with Jab

Star Jump with
Shoulder Press

Squat & Lift

Squat & Tap

Walk Ball through Legs & Sit

LEVEL 3 STRENGTH
SET C - LEGS

LUNGE ON THE BALL

1 With the ball behind you, place your foot on the ball. Keeping balance, roll the ball further behind you so that your front foot is three foot lengths in front of the ball. Ensure that your weight is centred over your front heel.

2 Inhale to lower, aiming to keep your hips in line with your knee so that you can just see your toes over your knee. Simultaneously raise your hands horizontally to the front.

3 Exhale, drawing your core muscles in and up and push up from your heel to the standing position, lowering your hands.

4 Lower for two counts, hold the lunge for three, and push up for two counts then repeat on the other leg.

SQUAT HOLD WITH SHOULDER PRESS

1 Stand with your feet parallel and hip width apart and sit your hips back so that your weight is over your heels. Hold the ball at chest level.

2 As you inhale, squat down aiming to lower your hips level with your knees so that you can just see your toes over your knees. Hold, drawing the core muscles in and up and press the ball above your head.

3 Exhale, as you push up from your heels, squeezing your glutes to the standing position.

4 Lower for two counts, hold the squat for three, and push up for two counts.

Level 3 Cardio Set D

Walk Forward Knee with Shoulder Press	x 2
Side Tap with Chest Press	x 8
Step Touch with Bounce	x 8
Double Step Touch with Full Circle & Skip	x 4
Squat & Knee	x 4

Walk Forward Knee
with Shoulder Press

Side Tap with
Chest Press

Step Touch with Bounce

Double Step Touch
with Full Circle & Skip

Squat and Knee

Level 3 Strength
Set D - Abdominals

Core Flexion with Double Leg Lower & Lift

1 Lie on your back on the floor, ball in hands reaching to the ceiling with legs in table-top position.

2 Draw your chin to your chest, curling up and forward. Make sure that you draw your core muscles in and up so that your lower back is not arching off the floor.

3 Inhale as you lower your heels to the floor keeping your knees bent, and exhale as you draw your core muscles in, raising your legs back to table-top position.

4 Lower your legs for two counts, hold for three and lift for two counts.

Overhead Reach with Double Leg Stretch

1 Lie on your back on the floor, in core flexion position with the ball over your shins.

2 Draw your core muscles in and up so that your back remains flat and is not arching.

3 Inhale as you reach your arms to your ears, stretching your legs forward at a 45-degree angle. Exhale, using your core muscles to draw back to the starting position.

4 Stretch out for two counts, hold for three, and draw in for two counts.

LEVEL 3 CARDIO SET E

BOUNCING WITH REACH & PULL	x 8
SIDE TAP WITH JAB	x 8
STAR JUMP WITH SHOULDER PRESS	x 8
SQUAT & LIFT (DOUBLE TIME)	x 8
(WALK AROUND BALL TO) SQUAT TAP	x 3
(WALK BALL THROUGH LEGS AND SIT)	
SQUAT & LIFT (DOUBLE TIME)	x 8
(WALK AROUND BALL TO) SQUAT TAP	x 3
(PICK UP THE BALL)	
WALK FORWARD KNEE WITH SHOULDER PRESS	x 2
SIDE TAP WITH CHEST PRESS	x 8
STEP TOUCH WITH BOUNCE	x 8
DOUBLE STEP TOUCH WITH FULL CIRCLE & SKIP	x 4
SQUAT & KNEE	x 4

LEVEL 3 STRENGTH SET E - TRICEPS

WALL DIPS

1 Place the ball on the floor against the wall, sit tall on the ball and place your hands close to your hips. Walk the feet forward and slide your hips off the ball.

2 Draw your core muscles in and up and pull up out of your shoulders and wrists.

3 Inhale, bending at your elbows so that your shoulders are at elbow level. Do not roll your shoulders forward. Exhale as you push up to the starting position.

4 Lower for two counts, hold the dip for three, and push up for two counts.

UNASSISTED DIPS

1 Place the ball on the floor, sit tall on the ball and place your hands close to your hips. Walk the feet forward and slide your hips off the ball.

2 For good balance, emphasise your core stability as you draw your core muscles in and up and pull up out of your shoulders and wrists.

3 Inhale, bending at your elbows so that your shoulders are at elbow level. Do not roll your shoulders forward. Exhale as you push up to the starting position.

4 Lower for two counts, hold the dip for three, and push up for two counts.

Cool Down & Stretch

The purpose of the cool down is to take the opportunity to stretch, increasing your flexibility and range of movement whilst your body is warm. Your increased flexibility will enable an improved performance of your cardiovascular and strength exercises in future workouts. Take this time to relax and wind down after you have worked at a high intensity.

Breathing

1 Lie on your back, legs elevated on the ball, arms by your side and palms to the floor. Draw shoulder blades down the back and keep your neck nice and long.

2 Inhale and expand your back on the mat. Exhale and draw the core muscles in and up (core muscles include transverse abdominus, obliques, rectus).

3 Inhale for three or four counts, then exhale for three or four counts.

4 Repeat twice more.

SPINAL ROTATION

1 From the previous position raise your arms in a horizontal position, palms down to the floor.

2 Inhale and roll the ball to one side. Go as far as you can whilst keeping both shoulder blades drawn down and on the floor.

3 Exhale, drawing core muscles in and up to return to centre.

4 Repeat three times on each side.

HIP & HAMSTRING STRETCH

1 From the previous position roll the ball away from you and cross the right ankle onto the left knee. Hold under the knee with both hands, reaching the left hand around the side and the right in between the legs, pressing the right knee open to feel the stretch in the hip.

2 Inhale to prepare, exhale as you stretch and press the knee away and stretch the hip.

3 Hold the stretch for three or four counts.

4 Extend the leg at the knee and point to the ceiling, placing your hands around your thigh, calf or ankle, depending on your flexibility.

5 Inhale to prepare, then exhale, drawing your leg towards your body allowing you to stretch your hamstring.

6 Hold the stretch for three to four counts.

7 Repeat on the other side.

Cool Down & Stretch

(continued)

Spinal Massage

1 From the previous position, pick the ball up with your feet and pass the ball to your hands, keeping your legs in the table-top position (knees over your hips, shins horizontal).

2 Draw your core muscles in and up.

3 Draw your chin to your chest, gently rocking forward and back three to five times, massaging the spine.

4 On your final rock forward, sit up and cross your legs.

Lower Back & Hip Stretch

1 From the previous position (legs crossed), roll the ball forward walking your hands down the ball. Draw your chin to your chest.

2 Inhale, extending from the lower back, exhale gently folding forward.

3 Hold for three or four counts.

4 Roll the ball slowly back to the original position.

Hamstring & Inner Thigh Stretch

1 Extend both legs to the side, pointing knees and toes to the ceiling.

2 Walk the ball forward gently, stretching the hamstring and adductor (inner thigh) muscles.

3 Inhale, draw in your core muscles in and up, exhale and stretch.

4 Hold the stretch for three to four counts and walk the ball back to the original position.

5 Repeat Lower Back & Hip Stretch on the other side.

Cool Down & Stretch

(continued)

Side Stretch

1 Sit on the floor with the ball to one side, in crossed legs position and place one arm on the ball.

2 Draw your core muscles in and up.

3 Inhale, lift your opposite arm up to your ear. While exhaling, increase the stretch over to the side.

4 Hold for three to four counts.

Neck Stretch

1 From the last position, draw your core muscles in and up to pull yourself into a seated position. Sit tall.

2 Inhale, placing your opposite hand over your head, and exhale, gently pulling your ear to your shoulder and stretching your neck.

3 Hold for three to four counts.

CHEST & SHOULDER STRETCH

1 Sitting tall in a crossed leg position, place the ball behind you. Aim to place both hands on either side of the ball.

2 Inhale, drawing your core muscles in and up.

3 Exhaling, squeeze your upper back together which will open your chest and shoulder.

4 Hold the stretch for three to four counts.

5 Bring the ball to the other side and repeat the Side Stretch and Neck Stretch on the other side.

CONCLUSION

*S*imply Ball & Band gives you the flexibility to train any time at home. Remember that practice makes perfect. To achieve maximum results and to realise the full benefits, it is advisable to be able to confidently perform each level before moving on to the next level. Optimal cardiovascular fitness and strength and endurance at each level will be realised when you can perform all the cardio blocks together, followed by all the strength training exercises, each without rest. You will then be well on your way to the next level. For the ultimate experience, join the cardiovascular workouts from level 1, 2, and 3, and likewise with the strength exercises. Perform all these without a rest.

At beginner level it is advisable to train twice a week. For those who would like to achieve their goals faster or who are advanced, training three to four times a week is conducive to reaching those results.

We give you our best wishes and hope you enjoy this workout and are soon realising the benefits as you naturally progress through the different levels, happily improving the quality of your life.

Stay fit, healthy and happy. Enjoy life!

Dina and Mark

GLOSSARY

BACK MUSCLES

A group of muscles located from the skull, down the spine, to the hip, attaching to the collarbone, shoulder blade and above the upper arm. They are responsible for depression (lowering), adduction (closer to the body) of the shoulder blades, extension (bringing back) and adduction of the upper arm at the shoulder joint.

BICEP

A muscle located at the shoulder blade and shoulder joint, going through the shoulder and elbow and attaching to the top of the forearm. It is responsible for flexion (bringing forward) of the upper arm at the shoulder joint, and flexion (bending) at the elbow.

CHEST MUSCLES

A group of muscles located at the sternum, collarbone and ribs that attach to the top of the upper arm and shoulder blades. They are responsible for horizontal flexion, flexion, adduction (closer to the body), internal rotation of the upper arm at the shoulder joint and depression (lowering), abduction (away from the body) and protraction (bringing forward) of the shoulder blades.

DRAWING THE CORE MUSCLES IN & UP - NAVEL/SPINE

The feeling of pulling the navel deep down internally and anchoring the back down to the floor as if there is a great weight pressing down, and drawing the tummy up underneath the rib cage.

GLUTEUS MAXIMUS AND MEDIUS

The group of muscles located at the pelvis attaching to the top of the thigh bone, responsible for extension (straightening), and the inward and outward turning of the upper leg at the hip joint.

HAMSTRINGS

The group of muscles located at the pelvis that run down the hip, the back of the thigh and knee attaching to the lower leg. They are responsible for flexion (straightening) at the hip and flexing the leg, bending at the knee joint.

HIP FLEXORS

Two muscles located at the hip, responsible for flexion (raising the upper leg) at the hip joint.

LENGTHENING

Conceptualising the body being pulled upward from the crown of the head, reaching out and extending from the spine.

OBLIQUES (EXTERNAL AND INTERNAL)

Side abdominal muscles located at the ribs and hip, responsible for flexion, side flexion and rotation in the torso.

QUADRICEPS

The group of muscles located at the hip running down the front of the thigh and attaching to the knee cap and above the shin. They are responsible for extending the leg, straightening at the knee joint.

RECTUS ABDOMINUS

The superficial abdominal muscles in the pelvis that attach to the ribs and sternum, responsible for flexion, side flexion and rotation of the trunk or spine.

TRANSVERSE ABDOMINUS

Deep abdominal muscles located at the hip and lower spine, attaching to the abdominal wall responsible for reducing the circumference of the abdomen, bracing the lower spine and drawing the abdominal region inward toward the spine.

TRICEPS

The group of muscles located at the shoulder blade and upper arm, running down the back of the shoulder, arms and through the elbow, attaching to the forearm. They are responsible for extension (bringing backward) of the upper arm at the shoulder and extension (straightening) of the arm at the elbow joint.

ABOUT THE AUTHORS

DINA MATTY

Dina is a trained dancer, aerobics champion and expert fitness teacher. Her study of dance in England led her to an exciting professional career that saw her on television and videos around the world. Dina then took up aerobics and became the UK and European champion over two years. She has since studied pilates and is passionate about the art and the benefits. Her studies under master teachers Romana Kryzanowska and Cynthia Lochard at the New York Pilates Studio in Sydney have made her dedicated to teaching Joseph H. Pilates' original format, and she is intent on furthering her studies to become a teacher trainer. Dina is now settled in Australia on the Gold Coast in Queensland where she is the proprietor of Pulse Health Studio in Niecon Tower in Broadbeach.

MARK RICHARDSON

Mark discovered martial arts in Japan at the age of six and became a student of Kyokushinkai Karate on the Gold Coast in Queensland at ten. His love of the art and his competition experience sparked an interest in boxing and other martial arts, developing a positive attitude and interest in health and fitness. Mark studied sports management and marketing at Griffith University and exercise science at the AIF. His studies have led him towards a career as a personal trainer alongside Dina at Pulse Health Studio in Niecon Tower in Broadbeach and as a karate instructor.

BOTH DINA AND MARK'S experience has previously given Dina the opportunity to present the DVD and book *Pilates the Authentic Way*, and Mark to present *Fighting Fit*. Now Dina and Mark are pleased to bring you their fitball and resistance band workout book and DVD *Simply Ball & Band*, and know that it will offer you a range of challenges whilst keeping the training fun. Look out for Dina and Mark in future releases in pilates, martial arts, and cardio and strength training, so that you can add to the variety of your overall health, fitness and well being.

SIMPLY
BALL & WEB

JULIA FILEP

For my two beautiful boys, Jacob and Connor, for every time they asked,
'Mummy, can you come and play?' and I answered, 'In a minute...'
For my husband Zoltan, who kept asking, 'Haven't you finished it yet?'
For my father Alex, for your tireless work on my house.
For my mother Margita and my mother-in-law Veronika for child care at the drop of a hat.

Julia Filep

Author: Julia Filep
Editor: Louise Coulthard
Art Director: Paul Scott
Photography: Ned Meldrum
Prepress: Graphic Print Group

Thanks to Albert Park Yacht Club

CONTENTS

INTRODUCTION   133
Precautions and safety, equipment

SET-UP TECHNIQUES   135
Seated position, supine bridge position,
floor bridge position

SEATED WARM-UP   137
Side band stretch, rotation stretch,
pelvic rocking, figure 8 pelvic rotations,
shoulder shrugs, shoulder circles

STANDING WARM-UP   141
Overhead lifts, overhead lift and squat,
squat tap, squat tap with rotations, standing
balance north and south, standing balance
east and west

CARDIO BOUNCE AND BALANCE   145
Cardio bounce and balance 1, cardio bounce
and balance 2, cardio bounce and balance 3,
cardio bounce and balance 4

CARDIO STANDING   153
Cardio standing 1, cardio standing 2,
cardio standing 3

MUSCLE CONDITIONING   161
Wall crawl, calf raises, the lift, ball push-ups,
abdominal curls, back extensions

RESISTANCE WEB EXERCISES   167
Give and take, triangle press, reach and
bend, ab crunches, obliques, ab stretch, tweezer
crunch, recover and stretch, rear deltoid press,
body roll, bicep curls, tricep overhead extensions,
gluteal extensions, gluteal orbits, gluteal presses

COOLDOWN AND STRETCH   183
Spinal rotation, lengthen and release,
adductor stretch, gluteal stretch, quadriceps

stretch, hip flexor stretch, spine stretch,
hamstring and calf stretch, bicep, shoulder
and chest stretch, tricep stretch,

GLOSSARY   189
CONCLUSION   191
ABOUT THE AUTHOR   192

INTRODUCTION

The fitness ball can be used in an extraordinary range of exercises that are suitable for all levels of fitness. Using the ball helps with:

• CORE AND SPINAL STABILITY. This refers to the strength and health of the spinal muscles (core muscles) that support the spine. These deep abdominal muscles partially wrap around the spine. They are important in maintaining good posture and caring for the back.

• BACK HEALTH. Exercising with the fitness ball strengthens the muscular structures responsible for spinal health and injury prevention.

• FITNESS AND BALANCE. Fitness ball exercise leads to improved cardiovascular fitness, respiratory system function and balance reactions.

Some people use a fitness ball instead of a chair. To remain balanced on the ball they must engage their abdominal and back muscles and maintain proper posture.

The resistance web adds another dimension to a ball workout. The resistance provided by the web improves strength, endurance and muscle condition. Resistance training also helps build bone strength and density, reduces body fat and leaves the body more toned.

PRECAUTIONS & SAFETY

DOCTOR'S CLEARANCE

Always consult a health professional before beginning an exercise program. If you have an illness, injury or disability or if you are pre- or post-natal it is especially important to consult with a health professional to establish that these exercises are suitable for you.

SAFETY TIPS

• Stop any exercise that causes pain. Don't be over-ambitious and work through pain; it is there to prevent serious damage.

• Stay well hydrated before, during and after exercise sessions.

• Avoid using the ball on slippery surfaces and near heaters, steps or sharp objects.

• Never hold your breath during the exercises.

HELPFUL HINTS

• The further the ball is from your body, the higher the degree of difficulty.

• Bringing your feet closer together makes it harder to balance, therefore increasing the challenge!

• Adding a bounce makes it more challenging.

EQUIPMENT

MAT

Cushioned fibre mats are available at sports stores and make floor exercises and stretches more comfortable. The ideal size is 60 cm (2 feet) wide and 180 cm (6 feet) long.

FITNESS BALL

The ball should have a diameter of around 55–85 cm (22–34 inches). It is used in many facets of exercise and physical therapy and is known by many different names, including body ball, exercise ball, fitball, gym ball, medi-ball, sports ball, stability ball, Swiss ball, therapy ball or yoga ball. It is much larger and lighter than a medicine ball.

RESISTANCE WEB

This innovative and flexible cord system suits most fitness balls. The resistance web will help strengthen your entire body with no-impact movement and resistance.

OPTIONAL EXTRA

A firm cushion is recommended if the floor or mat feels uncomfortable and it is difficult to maintain a seated position. It can also support your neck or back during some of the exercises and stretches.

SET-UP TECHNIQUES

These three key starting positions form the foundations of the exercises. They need to be mastered to ensure a safe, sound and effective workout.

SEATED POSITION

Focus: Core control and balance

1 Sit on top of or slightly forward of the ball. Your knees and hips should be at 90 degrees. Avoid slouching and maintain a tall, stable seated position on the ball.

2 Draw the belly button in to your spine by tensing the abdominal muscles. (Imagine you are a boxer in a boxing ring about to be hit in the belly. Protect your stomach by contracting your abdominals!)

3 React to the ball's movements with your pelvis to focus on core and spinal stability.

INCREASE THE CHALLENGE

Move your feet closer together. This narrows your base of support.
When you master this, try closing your eyes!

FLOOR BRIDGE POSITION

Focus: Core control, gluteal, spinal and hamstring strength and gluteal tone

1 Lie on your back with your heels and calves resting on the ball. Place your arms at your sides, palms facing down.

2 Tighten your buttocks and slowly lift your hips off the floor as you push down through your feet.

INCREASE THE CHALLENGE

Bring your feet closer on the ball.
Cross your arms across your chest so that your elbows are off the floor.

SUPINE BRIDGE POSITION

Focus: Core control and spinal, gluteal and quadriceps strength

1 Sit on the ball and walk your feet forward as you lean back on to the ball. Continue to walk away from the ball until your shoulders come to rest on it.

2 Your head and neck should feel comfortable on the ball and your knees should be directly above your ankles. If your chin is on your chest, walk your feet back a little.

3 To hold this position, press through your heels and squeeze your gluteals to keep your hips up.

INCREASE THE CHALLENGE

Bring your feet closer together to further strengthen your stabilisers.

SEATED WARM-UP

The purpose of warming up is to prepare your body for the exercises to come. It is also the perfect time for mental preparation. It's a good idea to leave behind the worries of the day and focus your thoughts on you and your workout.

SIDE BEND STRETCH

1 Sit up in the seated position. Look straight ahead and rest your hands on your thighs.

2 Tilt your right ear towards your right shoulder and hold for 1–2 breaths.

3 Return upright, then repeat on the left side.

4 Repeat the sequence at least 4 times.

ROTATION STRETCH

1 Maintaining the seated position, turn your head slowly to the right and hold for 1–2 breaths.

2 Return to the centre, then turn to the left and hold for 1–2 breaths.

3 Repeat the sequence at least 4 times.

If you still feel tense or stiff, repeat these exercises again.

SEATED WARM-UP

(continued)

PELVIC ROCKING

1 Sit tall on the ball in the seated position with your hands on your hips.

2 Roll the ball backward by rolling the hips forward, with a slight arch in the lower back.

3 Return to the starting position and then roll the ball forward by rolling the hips backward.

4 This completes 1 set. Perform 8-10 sets.

FIGURE 8 PELVIC ROTATIONS

1 Begin in the seated position with your hands on your hips.

2 Draw a figure 8, initiating the movement from your hips.

3 Draw the figure 8 clockwise 8 times and then anti-clockwise 8 times.

4 This completes 1 set. Perform 2-4 sets.

The movements in the next two exercises mobilise and prepare the shoulder muscles. If done regularly, they can help increase mobility and enhance your postural awareness.

SHOULDER SHRUGS

Shoulder shrugs encourage your chest to open because they relax your shoulder muscles. Tense shoulders cause a rounded upper back and lead to poor posture.

1 Begin in the seated position. Relax your shoulders and place your hands at your sides on the ball.

2 Slowly lift both shoulders up towards your ears. Hold this position for 2 counts and then lower down.

3 Repeat this 8 times up and down.

SHOULDER CIRCLES

1 Begin in the seated position.

2 Slowly lift and roll your shoulders back, drop them down and return to the starting position. Repeat 8–10 times.

3 Now perform the circle again, but this time roll your shoulders forward, drop them down and return to the starting position. Repeat 8–10 times.

STANDING WARM-UP

These exercises are performed in the standing position while holding the ball.

OVERHEAD LIFTS

1 Begin by holding the ball in front of your stomach with both hands on each side of the ball.

2 Keeping the shoulders relaxed, lift the ball above your head.

3 Slowly bring the ball down to the starting position. Ensure the ball and your elbows remain in your peripheral vision.

4 **Repeat this sequence 8 times.**

OVERHEAD LIFT AND SQUAT

1 Stand tall with your feet wide, holding the ball in front of you. Lift the ball above your head.

2 Bend your knees and lower the ball towards the floor, keeping your back straight and upright.

3 Straighten your legs and reach up again.

4 **Repeat this sequence 8 times.**

STANDING WARM-UP

(continued)

SQUAT TAP

1 Stand tall with your feet slightly wider than hip-width apart. Hold the ball in front of your stomach. Take a small squat down and push off to the right side. Tap the left toe down to the floor.

2 Repeat the squat down and push off to the left side. Tap the right toe down to the floor.

3 This is 1 repetition. Repeat this sequence 8–10 times.

INCREASE THE CHALLENGE
Hold the ball further out in front of you.

SQUAT TAP WITH ROTATIONS

1 As you execute the squat tap to the right side, rotate your torso to the right. The ball follows through to the right side.

2 Repeat the squat tap to the left side, and rotate your torso to the left. The ball follows through to the left side.

3 This is 1 repetition. Repeat this sequence 8–10 times.

INCREASE THE CHALLENGE
Hold the ball further out in front of you.

STANDING BALANCE NORTH AND SOUTH

1 Stand behind the ball. Place your right heel on the ball. Balance carefully with your left foot supporting you.

2 Slowly roll the ball forwards and backwards under your right heel. Run your arms beside you to help keep your balance. Repeat 8 times with your right foot.

3 Swap sides and repeat 8 times with your left foot.

STANDING BALANCE EAST AND WEST

1 Stand behind the ball. Place your right heel on the ball. Balance carefully with your left foot supporting you.

2 Slowly roll the ball sideways from left to right and back again. Run your arms beside you to help keep your balance. Repeat 8 times with your right foot.

3 Swap sides and repeat 8 times with your left foot.

CARDIO BOUNCE AND BALANCE

All the routines in both cardio sections consist of two components. Each exercise has movements that are performed with the lower half of the body, either while sitting on the ball or standing, and arm movements. Each routine can be repeated for 1–4 sets. The more sets performed, the greater the exercise intensity.

CARDIO BOUNCE AND BALANCE 1

Carry out the following exercise while performing seated-bouncing on the ball. Begin in the seated position.

HANDS ON HIPS

1 Sit with hands on hips. Keep shoulders relaxed, eyes forward, abdominals braced and chest lifted.

2 Bounce on the ball 8 times.

BOUNCE AND LIFT OFF

1 Begin in the seated position. Rest your hands beside you on the ball.

2 Bounce for a set number of repetitions and then lift off your buttocks. Support yourself with the right hand resting on the ball.

3 Pause for a moment with the buttocks off the ball.

4 Return to a bounce for the same number of repetitions and then lift off your buttocks. Support yourself with the left hand resting on the ball. This is one set.

5 Repeat, alternating hands with each lift off.

Perform the following routine incorporating these exercises.

8 hands on hips
4 bounces and lift offs, with
3 bounces between each lift off.
Repeat this sequence for 3 sets.

4 hands on hips
4 bounces and lift offs, with
2 bounces between each lift off.
Repeat this sequence for 3 sets.

4 hands on hips
4 bounces and lift offs, with
1 bounce between each lift off.
Repeat this sequence for 3 sets.

As you decrease the number of bounces between the lift off, the intensity will increase.

CARDIO BOUNCE AND BALANCE 2

Carry out the following arm exercises while performing seated-bouncing on the ball. Begin in the seated set-up position.

HANDS ON HIPS

1 Sit on the ball with hands on hips. Keep shoulders relaxed, eyes forward, abdominals braced and chest lifted.

2 Bounce on the ball 8 times.

CROSS AND PULL

1 Begin with your elbows by your sides.

2 Bring both hands up, crossing your wrists in front of your chest.

3 Pull both hands down to the starting position.

4 Perform the cross and pull movement in time with each bounce. Repeat 8 times.

OVERHEAD AND PULL

1 Relax your shoulders and keep your elbows beside your body.

2 Lift your arms above your head as you bounce.

3 Lower your arms and bounce. Ensure your hands remain in your peripheral vision. Repeat 8 times.

Repeat the entire sequence, performing 4 repetitions, then 2 and then 1 of each arm movement instead of 8.

PROGRESSION

Repeat the whole sequence again, replacing the bouncing with heel digs.

HEEL DIGS

1 Set up in the seated position. Keep your hands on your hips to help centre the body over the ball.

2 Tap the right heel out to the front as you take a bounce.

3 Bring the right foot back to the starting position with next bounce. It should take you 2 bounces to complete one side.

4 Tap the left foot out to the front with the next bounce.

5 Bring the left foot back to the starting position with next bounce. It should take a total of 4 bounces to complete both sides.

INCREASE THE CHALLENGE
Elevating the knees higher during this exercise will increase the intensity.

CARDIO BOUNCE AND BALANCE 3

Carry out the following arm exercises while performing seated-bouncing on the ball. Begin in the seated set-up position.

HANDS ON HIPS

1 Sit with hands on hips. Keep shoulders relaxed, eyes forward, abdominals braced and chest lifted.

2 Bounce on the ball 8 times.

MONKEY SWINGS

1 Relax your shoulders and bend slightly at the elbows.

2 As you bounce, swing the right arm up and the left arm down. Swing the arms alternately up and down.

3 Alternate the arms with each bounce. Repeat 8 times.

CLAP UP AND FRONT

1 Relax your shoulders and bend slightly at the elbows.

2 Clap once above your head and then once in front of your chest.

3 With each bounce, alternate the arms from above the head to in front of the chest. Repeat 8 times.

Repeat the entire sequence, performing 4 repetitions, then 2 and then 1 of each arm movement instead of 8.

PROGRESSION

Repeat the whole sequence again, replacing the bouncing with gumboot marching.

GUMBOOT MARCHING

1 Set up in the seated position.

2 Bounce on the ball, looking straight ahead.

3 With each bounce, alternately elevate each foot off the floor as if you are marching. Imagine you have big gumboots on your feet as you march.

INCREASE THE CHALLENGE
Elevating the knees higher during this exercise will increase the intensity.

CARDIO BOUNCE AND BALANCE 4

SIDE TAPS

1 Keep your hands on your hips to help centre the body over the ball.

2 Tap the right foot out to the right side as you take a bounce.

3 Bring the right foot back to the starting position with the next bounce.

4 Tap the left foot out to the left side as you take a bounce.

5 Bring the left foot back to the starting position with the next bounce. Continue to alternate the feet with each bounce.

Carry out the following arm exercises while performing side taps.

HANDS ON HIPS

1 Sit with hands on hips. Keep shoulders relaxed, eyes forward, abdominals braced and chest lifted.

2 Bounce on the ball 8 times.

BICEP CURLS

1 Relax your shoulders and keep your elbows beside your body. Make a relaxed fist with both hands.

2 Bend at the elbows and bring the fists up towards the shoulders.

3 Slowly lower down the fists back to the starting position.

4 The arms curl up with the first bounce and then down with the second bounce. Your elbows must remain under the shoulders throughout this movement. Repeat 8 times.

CROSS AND PULL

1 Begin with your hands by your sides.

2 Bring both hands forward and cross the wrists in front of your chest.

3 Return your hands back to the starting position.

4 Do this in sequence with each bounce. Repeat 8 times.

OVERHEAD AND PULL

1 Relax your shoulders and keep your elbows beside your body.

2 Lift your arms above your head as you bounce.

3 Lower your arms and bounce. Ensure your hands remain in your peripheral vision. Repeat 8 times.

4 Repeat the entire sequence, performing 4 repetitions, then 2 and then 1 of each arm movement instead of 8.

PROGRESSION

Repeat the whole sequence again, replacing the side taps with double side taps.

DOUBLE SIDE TAPS

1 Tap the right foot out to the right side as you take a bounce.

2 Bring the right foot back to the middle with the next bounce.

3 Tap the right foot out to the right side again as you take a bounce.

4 Bring the right foot back to the middle with the next bounce.

5 Tap the left foot out to the left side as you take a bounce.

6 Bring the left foot back to the middle with the next bounce.

7 Tap the left foot out to the left side again as you take a bounce.

8 Bring the left foot back to the middle with the next bounce.

CARDIO STANDING

CARDIO STANDING 1

Perform 8 step touches while holding the ball in front of you.

STEP TOUCH

1 Begin by standing tall with the feet together. Draw the shoulders back and lift the chest.

2 Take a single step to the right side and step the left leg in, meeting the legs together.

3 Take a single step to the left side and step the right leg in, meeting the legs together. Keep the body centred without leaning over to the side.

Carry out the following arm exercises while performing step touches.

OVERHEAD LIFT

1 Begin by holding the ball with both hands in front of your chest.

2 Elevate the ball above your head, bracing your core as you do this.

3 Bring the ball back to the starting position. Repeat 8 times.

Cardio Standing 1

(continued)

Push and Pull

1 Begin by holding the ball in both hands in front of your chest.

2 Extend the arms away from the chest as if you were pushing the ball away.

3 Bring the ball back to the starting position. Take care not to lock the elbows. Repeat 8 times.

Repeat the entire sequence, performing 4 repetitions, then 2 and then 1 of each arm movement instead of 8.

Increase the Challenge
Take wider and deeper steps.

Progression

Repeat the whole sequence again, replacing the step touches with step curls.

Step Curl

1 Begin by standing tall with the feet together. Draw the shoulders back and lift the chest.

2 Take a single step to the right side and curl the left leg up towards your buttocks.

3 Take a single step to the left side and curl the right leg up towards your buttocks.

CARDIO STANDING 2

Perform 8 step touches while holding the ball in front of you.

STEP TOUCH

1 Begin by standing tall with the feet together. Draw the shoulders back and lift the chest.

2 Take a single step to the right side and step the left leg in, meeting the legs together.

3 Take a single step to the left side and step the right leg in, meeting the legs together. Keep the body centred without leaning over to the side.

Carry out the following arm exercises while performing step touches.

SWINGING LOW

1 Start by holding the ball with both hands down in front of your thighs.

2 Like a pendulum, swing the ball down from right to left then left to right.

3 Keep your back upright and your eyes looking forward. Repeat 8 times.

Swinging High

1 Start by holding the ball with both hands down in front of your thighs.

2 Arching overhead, swing the ball from right to left, then left to right.

3 Keep your back upright and your eyes looking forward. Your elbows return to the ribs with each swing. Repeat 8 times.

Repeat the entire sequence, performing 4 repetitions, then 2 and then 1 each arm movement instead of 8.

Progression

Repeat the whole sequence again, replacing the step touches with step curls.

Step curl

1 Begin by standing tall with the feet together. Draw the shoulders back and lift the chest.

2 Take a single step to the right side and curl the left leg up towards your buttocks.

3 Take a single step to the left side and curl the right leg up towards your buttocks.

CARDIO STANDING 3

Perform 8 step touches while holding the ball in front of you.

STEP TOUCH

1 Begin by standing tall with the feet together. Draw the shoulders back and lift the chest.

2 Take a single step to the right side and step the left leg in, meeting the legs together.

3 Take a single step to the left side and step the right leg in, meeting the legs together. Keep the body centred without leaning over to the side.

Carry out the following arm exercises while performing step touches.

BOUNCE AND CATCH

1 Hold the ball in front of your torso.

2 Using both hands, allow the ball to bounce in front of you.

3 As the ball bounces up, be sure to catch the ball. This will test your reaction time and co-ordination. Repeat 8 times.

THROW AND CATCH

1 Hold the ball in front of you with both hands.

2 Throw the ball above your head.

3 Catch with both hands and return to starting position. Repeat 8 times.

Repeat the entire sequence, performing 4 repetitions, then 2 and then 1 of each arm movement instead of 8.

PROGRESSION

Repeat the whole sequence again, replacing the step touches with step curls.

STEP CURL

1 Begin by standing tall with the feet together. Draw the shoulders back and lift the chest.

2 Take a single step to the right side and curl the left leg up towards your buttocks.

3 Take a single step to the left side and curl the right leg up towards your buttocks.

MUSCLE CONDITIONING

WALL CRAWL

Focus: Thighs and buttocks

1 Position the ball against a wall between your mid and lower spine. Keep your back upright with your hands on your thighs for balance. Lean into the wall a little.

2 With your feet shoulder-width apart, slowly squat until your hips are at the same level as your knees, so your thighs are parallel with the floor. Hold this position for 2 counts.

3 Slowly stand back upright to the starting position. Focus your thoughts on your thigh muscles, as this will help to maximise the effect of the exercise.

4 Complete 8-12 reps. This makes up 1 set. Perform 1-3 sets.

DECREASE THE CHALLENGE
Try squatting at only a 45° angle. Decrease the amount of repetitions or perform only one set.

INCREASE THE CHALLENGE
Hold your position at the bottom of the squat for 4–6 counts and return to the top. Continue the repetitions with no rest between sets.

Muscle Conditioning

(continued)

Calf Raises

Focus: Calf strength and balance

1 Position the ball against a wall and lean against the ball with your chest, holding the sides with your hands.

2 Keeping the feet shoulder-width apart, raise yourself up on to your toes by lifting your heels. Hold this position for 2 counts.

3 Slowly lower yourself back down, placing your heels on the ground.

4 Complete 5-10 reps. This makes up 1 set. Perform 1-3 sets.

Decrease the Challenge
Decrease the amount of repetitions or perform only one set.

Increase the Challenge
Lift one leg off the ground and raise yourself up on to your toes using your supporting leg. Repeat with the other leg.

THE LIFT

Focus: Hamstrings and buttocks

1 Lie on your back with your heels and calves resting on the ball, toes relaxed and arms at your sides with palms facing down. Avoid locking your knees and keep your legs straight.

2 Squeeze your buttocks together and slowly lift your hips off the floor while pushing your heels down on to the ball.

3 Hold this position for 2 counts, then slowly lower your hips to the floor.

4 Complete 8-12 reps. This makes up 1 set. Perform 1-3 sets.

INCREASE THE CHALLENGE
Perform the exercise with your arms raised toward the ceiling or, alternatively, with your hands clasped over your stomach. This reduces your basis of support, challenging your balance.

DECREASE THE CHALLENGE
Keep the ball closer to your buttocks and place your hands out wider on the floor to increase your basis of support.

Muscle Conditioning

(*CONTINUED*)

Ball Push-ups

Focus: Chest

1 Begin by kneeling on the floor, then roll forward over the ball. Walk your arms forward until your thighs are on the ball.

2 Bend your elbows, slowly lowering your chest to the floor until your chin nearly touches the floor. Hold for 2 counts.

3 Push back up slowly. Avoid locking the elbows at the top.

4 Complete 8-12 reps. This makes up 1 set. Perform 1-3 sets.

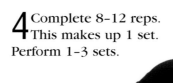

Increase the Challenge
Walk your hands further away from the ball until your shins or even your toes are on the ball.

Decrease the Challenge
Begin with the ball under your hips.

ABDOMINAL CURLS

Focus: Abdominals and back

1 Lie on your back in the supine bridge position. Walk your feet back until the ball is under your lower back and pelvis. Cross your arms over your chest and keep your knees above your ankles.

2 Elevate your shoulders off the ball, about half-way between lying and sitting. Make sure you keep the pelvis and tailbone in contact with the ball.

3 Slowly roll back down to your starting position.

4 Complete 8-12 reps. This makes up 1 set. Perform 1-3 sets.

DECREASE THE CHALLENGE
Take a small step forward. This will give more support to your neck and upper back area. Keep bracing through the gluteals.

INCREASE THE CHALLENGE
Take a step backward. Bring your feet closer together.

BACK EXTENSIONS

Focus: Abdominals and back

1 Lie with your stomach and hips on the ball, and your chest, head and neck raised. Keep your feet apart, your hands at your sides and your head in line with your spine. Push your feet down for support.

2 Keeping your neck long, raise your chest slightly.

3 Lower back to the starting position.

4 Complete 8-12 reps. This makes up 1 set. Perform 1-3 sets.

RESISTANCE WEB EXERCISES

SET-UP POSITION

1 Begin by sitting on the floor with the ball at your back. Ensure both 'D' rings are at the sides of your body.

2 Place your palms through the handles and relax your grip. Cross your legs and sit up tall.

3 Avoid holding your breath. Always use your breath to firm your abdominals and support your posture.

4 Ensure that you control the return phase of each exercise.

If you find it difficult to maintain this position, sit on a firm cushion.

GIVE AND TAKE

Focus: Chest and shoulders

1 With your elbows at your sides and your palms up, press out, keeping your shoulders down.

2 Pause for 2–4 counts and then return.

3 Use your abdominal muscles to support the length of your spine. Maintain a rhythmic breath.

4 Complete 8–12 reps. This makes up 1 set. Perform 1–3 sets.

DECREASE THE CHALLENGE
Reduce the number of repetitions. Reduce the time taken to pause before the return.

RESISTANCE WEB EXERCISES

(continued)

TRIANGLE PRESS

Focus: Chest and shoulders

1 Lift your elbows and keep your shoulders down. Reach your arms as if you were hugging. Keep your shoulders down and your elbows lifted.

2 Pause for 2–4 counts and return.

3 Keep your breastbone lifted without pushing your ribcage forward. Keep the band under your elbows throughout the sequence, otherwise you will pull the ball over your head.

4 Complete 8-12 reps. This makes up 1 set. Perform 1-3 sets.

INCREASE THE CHALLENGE
Reduce the number of repetitions.
Reduce the time taken to pause before the return.

DECREASE THE CHALLENGE
Increase the pause to 6–8 counts.
Combine give and take and triangle press. For example, perform 1 repetition of each for 8 sets.

SET-UP POSITION

1 Hold the right strap in your right hand and move the ball so that the 'D' ring is toward the top of the ball. Place your feet evenly on the floor and sit tall on the ball.

REACH AND BEND

Focus: Obliques and upper back

1 Extend your right hand above your head. Keeping your shoulders down, bend to the right, going up and over.

2 Return to the centre. Allow your head to follow the arch of your spine. Use your exhalation to stabilise your core. Repeat 8–12 times.

3 Change sides and repeat the sequence.

4 Complete 8-12 reps on each side. This makes up 1 set. Perform 1-3 sets.

INCREASE THE CHALLENGE
Bring your feet closer together. This narrows your base of support.

Resistance Web Exercises

(continued)

Set-up position

1 Sit evenly with the 'D' rings equally distanced from the floor.

2 Walk your feet out so that the ball is supporting your lower back.

3 Bend your elbows and place them in a 'stick 'em up' position.

Ab Crunches

Focus: Abdominals

1 Pull your abdominals in and pulse up. Keep your shoulders down and your movements smooth. Initiate the movement from your abdominal muscles, not your head.

2 Return back to the starting position. Ensure the straps stay over the elbows during the exercise.

3 Complete 8–12 reps. This makes up 1 set. Perform 1–3 sets.

OBLIQUES

Focus: Abdominals and obliques

1 Pulse up, moving your right shoulder towards the left knee. Twist from your torso, pulling your abs in. Keep the back of your neck long.

2 Return to the starting position. Ensure the straps stay over the elbows during the exercise.

3 Repeat the sequence, this time moving your left shoulder towards your right knee.

4 Complete 8–12 reps of the entire sequence. This makes up 1 set. Perform 1–3 sets.

RESISTANCE WEB EXERCISES

(continued)

AB STRETCH

Focus: Abdominals

1 Release the straps and place your hands behind your neck for support. Slowly straighten your legs to a comfortable position.

2 Lie back over the ball, so that your back is curled over the ball and your head is resting on the ball.

3 Let your elbows relax apart and allow the ball to support your spine. Allow your arms to fall down beside the ball.

4 Consciously relax the body and breath. You will feel a stretch in your abdominal muscles. Hold the stretch for 20–60 seconds.

SET-UP POSITION

1 Lie on your back and bend your knees. Place the ball between your feet.

2 Grasp the handles and extend your arms straight.

3 Place your feet behind the 'D' rings. Squeeze your feet to keep the ball in position and lift your feet towards the ceiling.

TWEEZER CRUNCH

Focus: Abs and inner thighs

1 Lift your head up and maintain this position with the shoulders off the floor.

2 Begin to pulse your arms with the palms facing down, as if you were bouncing a ball. Continue breathing at all times. Keep the lower ribs engaged and your neck long.

3 Complete 8-12 reps. This makes up 1 set. Perform 1-3 sets.

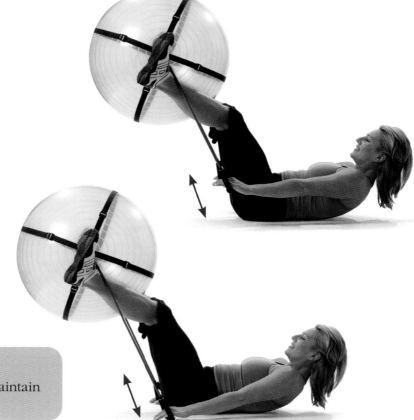

INCREASE THE CHALLENGE
Elevate your shoulders higher and maintain this position during the arm pulses.

RESISTANCE WEB EXERCISES

(continued)

SET-UP POSITION

1 Sitting in an upright position, place the ball in front of you.

2 Stretch out your legs on either side of the ball.

RECOVER AND STRETCH

Focus: Abs and inner thighs

1 Lean forward and place the palms of your hands on top of the ball.

2 Relax your breath and lean forward, allowing your stomach and inner thighs to stretch. Hold the stretch for 20–60 seconds and release.

SET-UP POSITION

1 While holding the straps, sit upright and place your feet in a 'V' position on the ball in front of you.

2 Extend your legs and keep the knees bent. Hold this position.

If you find it difficult to maintain this position, sit on a firm cushion.

REAR DELTOID PRESS

Focus: Back, abs, buttocks and arms

1 Bend your arms out to the sides and raise them out at right angles. Keep the elbows below shoulder level.

2 Draw the elbows behind the back as if you were squeezing a ball between your shoulder blades.

3 Hold for 2–4 counts and then return.

4 Complete 8-12 reps. This makes up 1 set. Perform 1-3 sets.

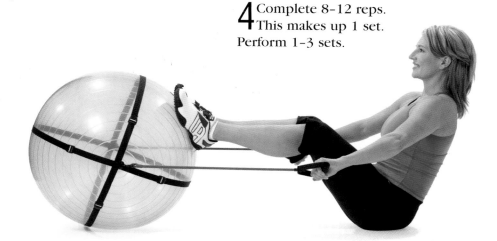

INCREASE THE CHALLENGE
Hold the straps below the handle, shortening them.

RESISTANCE WEB EXERCISES

(continued)

BODY ROLL

Focus: Back, abs, buttocks and arms

1 Bring your hands together at your middle, keeping your elbows out wide and your shoulders down.

2 Roll your body back into a 'C' shape and hold for 1–2 breaths.

3 Roll back to a long spine and then return to the set-up position.

4 Complete 8–12 reps. This makes up 1 set. Perform 1–3 sets.

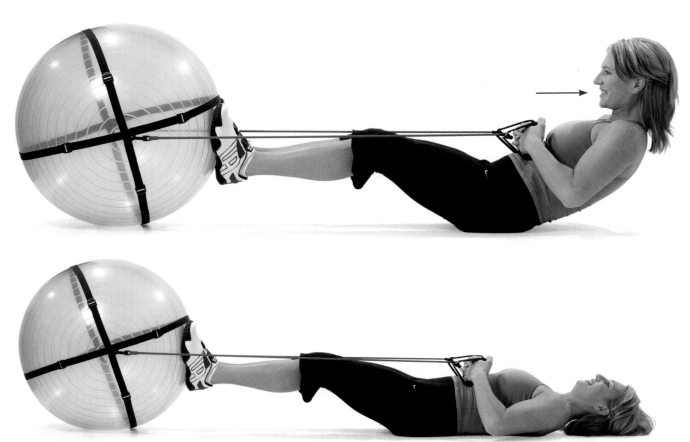

BICEP CURLS

Focus: Back, abs, buttocks and arms

1 Start in the set-up position.

2 Roll back so your shoulders and head are off the ground, and then hold. Draw your elbows into your sides and keep your palms up.

3 Curl your arms up towards your face and then return. Elbows must remain fixed beside the body.

4 Complete 8–12 reps. This makes up 1 set. Perform 1–3 sets.

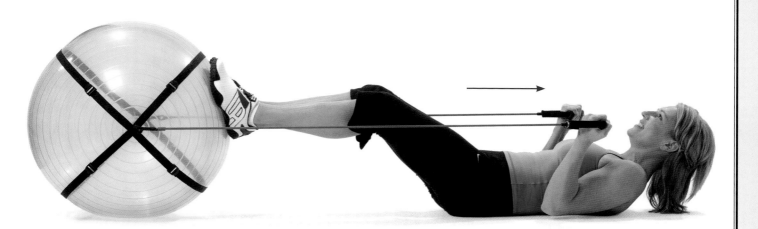

INCREASE THE CHALLENGE
Add 2–4 pulses at the top of the curl for each repetition.

RESISTANCE WEB EXERCISES

(continued)

SET-UP POSITION

1 Begin in the seated position on the ball.

2 Your hips and knees should be at a 90 degree angle.

TRICEP OVERHEAD EXTENSIONS

Focus: Back, abs, buttocks and arms

1 Sit tall, clasping the handles together. Elevate both your hands behind your head, with elbows bent and in full view, and hands clasped behind your head. Tuck your upper arms in towards your ears.

2 Slowly raise the hands above the head and then slowly return to the starting position. Your elbows must remain in full view and tucked in.

3 Complete 8-12 reps. This makes up 1 set. Perform 1-3 sets.

INCREASE THE CHALLENGE
Add 2–4 pulses at the top of the extension for each repetition.

DECREASE THE CHALLENGE
Reduce the range of motion by only extending the hands half way.

SET-UP POSITION

1 Kneel beside the ball with the 'D' ring in front of your supporting leg.

2 Place your opposite foot in the strap and lie sideways over the ball.

3 Brace your abs and extend your strapped leg straight out to the side. Keep the foot flexed and your body in a straight line from your head to your toes.

GLUTEAL EXTENSIONS

Focus: Buttocks and thighs

1 From the starting position, extend your leg forward to the front, keeping it straight out from your hip. Keep your body stable and move only your leg. Control the movement from your abs.

2 Add a pulse and then bring your leg back to the starting position.

3 Complete 8–12 reps. This makes up 1 set. Perform 1–3 sets.

INCREASE THE CHALLENGE
Pause and hold the leg to the rear for 2–4 counts.

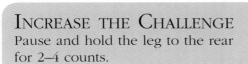

RESISTANCE WEB EXERCISES

(continued)

GLUTEAL ORBITS

Focus: Buttocks and thighs

1 Hold the leg out to the side in the set-up position and point your toes.

2 Make small circles with your leg, keeping your body stable and moving only your leg.

3 Repeat with the other leg.

4 Complete 8–12 reps. This makes up 1 set. Perform 1–3 sets.

> ### INCREASE THE CHALLENGE
> Reverse the circles with the same number of repetitions.

SET-UP POSITION

1 Kneeling on the floor, place the 'D' ring so that it is on the side of the ball.

2 Lie over the ball with your foot through the handle and your hands on the floor under your shoulders.

GLUTEAL PRESSES

Focus: Buttocks and thighs

1 Pull your abs in and lift your leg to a straightened position.

2 Pulse the leg above the line of the body and lower your leg. Perform 8–12 reps.

3 Perform the sequence again with the other leg. Perform 8–12 reps.

4 This makes up 1 set. Perform 1-3 sets.

COOLDOWN AND STRETCH

Regular stretching helps improve your mobility and flexibility, particularly as you age, and reduces your chances of injury. Stretching after exercise is vital as the muscles are receptive when warm. It will help to lengthen your muscles and to disperse any lactic acid that forms during your exercise session.

Stretching is not competitive so only stretch as far as you are comfortable. Stretching is a natural tranquilliser and will generate a serene sense of well-being, so relax and enjoy!

Remove the web from the fitness ball before commencing the cooldown.

SPINAL ROTATION

1 Lie on your back with your knees bent, holding the ball on the floor behind your head.

2 Roll your knees to one side and the ball to the other. Relax your stomach and spine and breathe deeply. Hold this stretch for 4–6 deep breaths.

3 Slowly roll your knees and the ball to the other sides and hold for 4–6 deep breaths.

4 Repeat twice on each side.

LENGTHEN AND RELEASE

1 Lie on your back and hold the ball behind your head, keeping your legs straight.

2 Stretch, aiming for maximum length from your fingers to your toes. Allow your lower back to arch off the floor.

3 Hold the stretch for 4–6 breaths, release and repeat again.

COOLDOWN AND STRETCH

(continued)

ADDUCTOR STRETCH

1 Lie on your back with your feet resting on the ball and your knees open to the sides. Keep the soles of your feet turned towards each other.

2 Roll the ball towards you, stretching your inner thighs. Hold the stretch for 4-6 breaths.

GLUTEAL STRETCH

1 Lie on your back with one foot and calf placed on top of the ball.

2 Place your opposite foot across your thigh just above the knee. Clasp your hands under the thigh of the leg resting on the ball.

3 Draw the ball in towards you until you feel a stretch in the buttocks of the top leg. Hold the stretch for 4 breaths and switch sides.

QUADRICEPS STRETCH

1 Begin by kneeling behind the ball.

2 Roll over the ball and walk out your hands until your hips are resting on the ball.

3 Draw your belly button in to your spine. Bring one heel towards your buttocks and hold your foot. Hold this position for 4–6 breaths and then release.

4 Repeat the exercise again, switching feet.

If you find it hard to balance, place your supporting hand and foot further out to the side.

HIP FLEXOR STRETCH

1 Sit upright on the ball and look straight ahead. Place your hands on top of your thighs as you brace your core.

2 Bring one leg round to the back of the ball and then straighten it. Push your hips forward and lean back slightly. Hold this position for 4–6 breaths and then release.

3 Repeat the exercise again, switching sides.

If you feel unbalanced, rest your hands on the sides of the ball.

COOLDOWN AND STRETCH

(continued)

SPINE STRETCH

1 Kneel on the floor in front of the ball.

2 Roll over the ball and walk your hands out until both hands and feet are touching the floor.

3 Allow your body to collapse over the ball. Hold this position for 4-6 breaths.

HAMSTRING AND CALF STRETCH

1 Sit on the ball with one leg outstretched with a slight bend in the knee.

2 Keeping your back straight, tilt forward from the hips and reach towards the ankle of the outstretched leg. Stop when you feel a stretch in the back of the upper leg.

3 Hold this stretch for 4-6 breaths and then repeat on your other leg.

Bicep, Shoulder and Chest Stretch

1 Sit upright on the ball and look straight ahead.

2 Clasp your hands together behind your lower back.

3 Straighten your arms as you push your hands away from your body. Feel your chest elevate and draw your shoulders down. Hold this position for 4-6 breaths.

Tricep Stretch

1 Sit upright on the ball and look straight ahead.

2 Draw in your belly button and raise your right arm above your head. Bend your arm backwards at the elbow and reach down your spine with your hand.

3 Place your left hand on the right elbow and gently press until you feel the stretch. Hold for 4-6 breaths and then repeat with the left arm.

GLOSSARY

ABDOMINALS
The sheet of muscles between the ribs and the hips.

ADDUCTORS
Muscles of the inner thighs running from the groin to the knee joint.

BICEPS
Muscles located at the front of the upper arm in the area between the elbow joint and the shoulder joint.

CALVES
The muscles of the rear lower leg situated between the knee joint and the ankle joint.

CORE
The group of deep internal muscles that brace and support the spine.

GLUTEALS
The muscles of the buttocks.

HAMSTRINGS
The muscles of the rear upper leg found between your buttocks and knee joints.

HIP FLEXORS
Bands of muscle that slide over the hips connecting the legs to the torso.

MOTOR PLANNING
The ability to automatically start, perform and complete a series of movements to achieve a desired outcome.

OBLIQUES
Side abdominal muscles that help the torso twist and rotate.

PELVIC/PELVIS
The area where the torso and legs join.

REPS AND SETS
A repetition (rep) is one complete cycle of an exercise from the starting position to the finishing position. Reps refers to the number of times to do an exercise. A set is a set amount of reps you should complete continuously without a rest.

TAILBONE
The bony end of the spine, located in the lower centre of the buttocks, also known as the coccyx bone.

TRICEPS
Located at the back of the upper arm between the elbow joint and the shoulder joint.

CONCLUSION

HOW EXERCISE CAN BENEFIT YOU

To enjoy life to the full it helps to be in good physical health. You don't have to train like an Olympic athlete to enjoy the benefits of exercise.

- Regular exercise helps you to expend energy. This is especially important for general well-being.

- Exercise helps to prevent the loss of muscle mass that often occurs through a lack of exercise and the ageing process.

- It increases your daily resting metabolism (the rate at which the body burns calories).

- Exercise can be done anywhere and you don't need to have access to gym equipment.

It's easy to talk about the benefits of exercise but the rewards only come from actually doing it!

CONTROLLING YOUR WEIGHT

The key to weight control is keeping energy intake (food) and energy output (physical activity) in balance. When you consume only as many calories as your body needs, your weight will usually remain constant. If you take in more calories than your body needs, you will put on excess fat. If you expend more energy than you take in, you will burn excess fat.

Exercise plays an important role in weight control by increasing energy output, calling on stored calories for extra fuel. Recent studies show that not only does exercise increase metabolism during a workout, but it causes your metabolism to stay increased for a period of time after exercising, allowing you to burn more calories.

Combining regular exercise with sensible nutrition is the best way to lose weight and improve health and fitness. Make the change. You won't be disappointed.

Keep active for the rest of your life!

ABOUT THE AUTHOR

Julia Filep has extensive experience in the health and fitness industry. She is a registered fitness leader and has over sixteen years teaching experience in all facets of freestyle group exercise. She also lectures and conducts VicFit accreditation modules as a teacher trainer in Geelong, Victoria.

Julia has hosted and participated in *Heat*, a personal fitness television series airing on cable television in Australia and overseas.

A mother of two small children, Julia enjoys the challenge of balancing exercise, work and family. Julia's genuine passion and enthusiasm for fitness and exercise is evident with the vast array of classes she teaches. Participants regularly rave about her teaching style and motivation. She is well known for her inspiring teaching style, getting the 'best/most' results out of her participants.